GU
.O47
1982
V.1

CHAMPIONSHIP
TRACK & FIELD

Volume 1:
TRACK EVENTS

---

edited by

JOHN RANDOLPH

Leisure Press
P.O. Box 3
West Point, N.Y. 10996

A publication of Leisure Press.
P.O. Box 3, West Point, N.Y. 10996
Copyright © 1982 Leisure Press
All rights reserved. Printed in the U.S.A

Library of Congress Number: 79-92134
ISBN O-918438-14-4

All Articles in the book used by permission of *The Athletic Journal.*

Cover design: Diana Goodin
Front cover photo: Don Gosney
Back cover photo: David Madison

CONTENTS

PART III: THE MIDDLE DISTANCES

PART IV: THE LONG DISTANCES AND CROSS COUNTRY

PART V: THE RELAYS

PREFACE

In selecting these articles from the pages of *The Athletic Journal*, I have attempted to provide a collection of materials that go beyond the boundaries of the typical text written for the track and field coach.

Instead, *Track and Field by the Experts* is a two-volume series designed to provide the coach with a wide array of *practical* knowledge and tools to enable him or her to help the athlete succeed.

A thorough background in technique studies is provided by the many "frame-by-frame" pictures of champions performing in each event. A number of different training philosophies and methods are also included. Here I have attempted to represent the many and varied ways that can produce winning results for the athlete.

Finally, by including a broad cross section of training ideas I have endeavored to encourage innovation and experimentation on the part of the coach. This is done in the belief that variety and ingenuity are integral parts of the total process of challenging and motivating athletes towards the realization of long range goals.

Track and Field by the Experts offers the coach and athlete many ingredients that can result in success. The selection and blend of these ingredients into a recipe for winning track and field is the challenge that awaits the reader.

John Randolph

PART I

THE SPRINTS

1

DEVELOPING A CHAMPION SPRINTER

Jim Bush, University of California/Los Angeles
and
Don Weiskopf, American River College

Speed, strength, relaxation, and the proper mental attitude are all essential factors in sprinting success, but if a runner does not possess natural speed, he will never be a champion sprinter. While we agree that sprinters, as a rule, are born and not developed, their speed can be improved through the effective execution of the basic mechanics of running and conditioning. A champion sprinter is the product of long training and practice.

An increase in leg strength is considered the most beneficial means of increasing stride length. For example, we have had sprinters who could not leg press 200 pounds. After regular training on gaining strength, they were able to leg press 200 pounds with explosion and speed. By improving leg, foot, and ankle strength, muscles will contract more swiftly and leg speed will be nearer maximum. Surely, sprinters such as Vasily Borzov, Don Quarrie, Reggie Jones and Ivory Crockett would not possess such powerful leg speed if their legs were not half as strong as they are.

The arms play an important role in running. Actually, the arms are as important as the legs since they help determine how long the running stride is. Arm action should be powerful, regular, and quick. For good leg drive, they must be driven with maximum power in a steady pumping action. If the runner can maintain good strength in his arms, his stride will remain more relaxed and smoother.

Unless the athlete develops the ability to run relaxed, he will never become an outstanding sprinter. Many of the sprinting greats appear to be loafing because they run so easily. Running is a pushing action, never a pulling action. During the driving phase, a runner should experience the

8

feeling of pushing the ground backward, away from him.

At UCLA, we are constantly looking for a powerful, explosive thrust of the driving or rear leg, ankle and foot. The stronger the force of the driving leg, the greater the stride length and the greater the thrust.

Coaching has often been over-emphasized. In many instances, too many of our athletes are overcoached. While I think it is an asset for a track athlete to have a great amount of knowledge and experience, a coach should be no more than a guide, a reference. The athlete should have an opportunity to develop his own style and not be molded to the coach's dream of how an athlete should look or how he feels an athlete should look. This has been a mistake made by track and field coaches.

The accompanying illustrations show an outstanding group of sprinters, including my three greatest quartermilers, world-record-holders, John Smith, Bennie Brown and Wayne Collett. Series A shows several UCLA sprinters, including Mike Bush, during a training drill on the start. Esther Rot, Israeli national record holder in the 80 meters hurdles and a finalist in the 1972 Olympic Games in Munich, trained with us at UCLA. Reggie Jones of Tennessee is one of America's fastest and most exciting sprinters. Mohinder Gill, now coaching at the University of Redlands, competed as a sprinter and also in his triple jump specialty for Cal Poly (San Luis Obispo) and his native India. The veteran, Don Quarrie, is recognized as one of the fastest human beings in the world.

Relaxation is the Key to Running

The key to good sprinting technique is running relaxed. Great sprinters appear relaxed as they dash down the track. Unfortunately, the typical young, inexperienced runner really does not know how to relax. At UCLA, this is the first thing for which I look. Considerable emphasis is placed on the technique of running relaxed. We are constantly looking for what is relaxing for the runner, and this is what we try to teach him, how to relax. While one set of muscles is working quickly, the opposing set must relax. If he runs tight in any part of his body, whether in the upper or lower part, the sprinter will tie up, which in turn will affect his legs.

Relaxation cannot be taught at a fast pace. A runner must learn how to relax at moderate speeds; otherwise, he will either become tied up or suffer pulled muscles. If he learns how to relax at a slow pace, he will become faster and faster as the year progresses. Furthermore, he should never have a pulled muscle. Usually a pulled muscle occurs when the athlete does something foolish the day before or he failed to warm up properly before the race.

How can a runner utilize a more relaxed style? If he is a new athlete, I watch him for three or four sessions before making any comments. I want to find out if the style which I think is wrong is actually relaxing for him, and a

1 **2**

3 **4**

5 **6**

Series A.

Esther Rot, Israeli national record holder in the 80 meters hurdles and a finalist in the 1972 Olympic Games in Munich.

coach cannot tell in one look. It is a mistake for a coach to take one look at an athlete and tell him what he is doing wrong.

Generally, I try to determine whether or not his shoulders are down and relaxed, not bunched up and tight. I do not care how he uses his arms as long as the arms, neck and shoulders appear relaxed. His jaws should be relaxed —sort of bouncing around.

Then I look for the knee lift. Some athletes cannot lift their knees too high. All the textbooks say that an athlete has to be a high knee lifter in order to be a good sprinter. This is not always true. Some athletes due to their body build cannot lift their knees too high. I want to check the type of body lean the runner has. Some lean too far forward, while others are too straight up and down, or lean backwards.

A sprinter should be up on his toes, getting full extension of his legs, and driving off his leg completely. There are so many different theories on how an athlete is supposed to run in order to get the most out of his body. Actually, I do not believe any theory is the answer. A coach has to take the athlete, look at him or her, and then decide what is best for the individual.

Emphasis on Quality, Not Quantity

When we start out in the fall, we go very slowly. However, all of our workouts are based on quality and not quantity. This is one point I emphasize continually to my athletes. In any field of endeavor, when an attempt is made to mix quality with quantity, the ingredient is destroyed.

Quality is what I want, so we do the same workouts from the start of school in September, five days a week, until June. But our runners become faster and faster. We keep telling the athletes, *Don't try to go too fast early in the year because you cannot learn how to relax. You will learn what is the best arm action for you, the proper knee lift, and the proper push-off. Until you get it at a slow speed, you do not realize these improvements, but every week you will become faster.*

For instance, it is difficult for a runner to lift his knees very high when he is going fast. When he goes slower, it is easier for the knees to come up. I tell a sprinter, *Lift your knees as high as you can, as long as they feel relaxed.* As he goes faster, the knees will go higher, If he tries to lift them too high when going slow, there is a tendency for him to be thrown backwards and to become tied up. Therefore, our sprinters are told, *Take just what you can handle.*

Starting. Quite often, a race is won or lost at the start. Therefore, correct starting technique should be a major area of concern to the coach and his sprinter. Since a sprinter must reach his top running speed quickly, he needs a start which will provide maximum acceleration. However, starting is something that a coach has to be very careful about. While his athletes have to work on starting to become good starters, a considerable amount of practice can induce injuries because it is the hardest thing on the body.

When the legs and arms are not synchronized properly and are not working together, sprinters are subject to pulled hamstring and groin muscles. Therefore, a coach cannot afford to have them take a great many starts because it takes too much out of his athletes. However, he has to work on starting until it is perfected. For this reason we do a number of form starts.

Many coaches make a mistake by trying to get their sprinters to explode out of the blocks. I do not like the work *explosive* any more. Instead, I prefer getting across to my athletes, *It is not exploding out of the blocks but it is running out of the blocks. When that gun goes off, you are going to go as fast as you can.*

The sprinters are told: *If you and another sprinter with equal speed explode out of the blocks and he is faster by 2 yards at the end of 10 yards, and then you are both together at the finish of 100 yards, what does that mean? It means that the man who exploded out of the blocks lost probably somewhere during the first 15, 25 or 30 yards because he pushed off so hard he could not synchronize his arms with his legs.*

As he reacts to the gun, the sprinter's arm should start to lift and his body should be driving out and up. It should always be driving out and up. Driving the opposite arm up helps bring the hips down into place, and he can get that straight line. The right leg should drive forward as the left leg achieves full extension.

In running out of the blocks, the sprinter cannot lift his knees too high. If he does, he will straighten up too quickly. This is an area in which the coach has to be very careful. True, we like to emphasize lifting the knees high, but only after the runner gets into his running position. If he tries to lift his knees too high when he is coming out from his start, he is brought into an upright position before he has really generated the power.

We never like to work on starts two days in a row. Starting is too hard on the legs. Neither do we like to work on starts two days before any meet. Sprinters should have two days to recover from starting practice.

Many coaches make the mistake of drilling so hard on who the first man is out of the blocks. It is more important to find out who is the first man at 20 yards.

Types of Starts. There are three basic types of starts which are named for the placement of the blocks: the bunched, the medium, and the elongated starts. They refer to the relative positioning of both the hands and feet. Generally, most sprinters use the medium start (Diagram I).

● **Bunch.** In the bunched start, the sprinter kneels with his toes on his back foot about the middle of his forward foot. Coaches who advocate the bunched start feel is is best because the runner is given an opportunity to uncoil with power and quickness. While the bunch start is fastest off the blocks for about 30 yards, it is not the fastest for the entire race. The sprinter's feet are close together. While this is generally true, there is a more difficult transition period when using this start.

To say that one type of start is better than the other is a mistake. If the bunch start is good for a short athlete with power and he has good transition from the start to running form, then that should be his start.

Since the hips are held high in a bunch start, the sprinter may have difficulty holding his position during a long set position. After leaving the blocks, this might cause him to stand upright to soon.

The great Jesse Owens used a bunch start, with the front block set only 8 inches from the line and the rear block another foot to the rear.

● **Medium.** Many authorities believe the medium start results in the fastest time for the entire race. This start is more comfortable than the bunch start and is popular among both men and women sprinters. It still allows the sprinter enough gather of muscle force for a quick explosion from the blocks.

Many coaches throughout the country favor this start. I like to start a beginner with the medium start and then go either to the elongated or the bunched, depending on his body build and what feels best for that athlete.

● **Elongated.** If he is tall, a sprinter may feel more comfortable with an elongated start. Most long-legged runners cannot start with the blocks close together because on the set position their hips would be too high.

Bud Winters of San Jose University has employed successfully the so-called *rocket* start, which is like the elongated style in which the body is stretched way back.

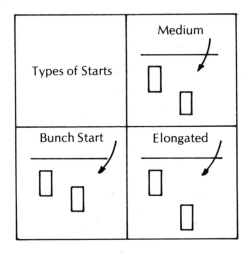

Diagram I

14

Taking the Marks. As he moves to the *On Your Marks* position, a sprinter should have his strongest leg back to initiate the movement, although most of his power comes from the front leg. Therefore, I instruct our sprinters to walk up to the starting line, pretend they are going to take a standing start, and then they put one leg back automatically. Usually, a sprinter will put the one back that he feels is the strongest or the most natural and comfortable from which to push off. Then we tell him, *All right, that is your back foot in the blocks.*

A sprinter can use any block setting that is correct and feels comfortable for him as long as he can feel pressure on the back block. The back leg is the one that initiates the start. The only way to determine the distance between the front and back blocks is to experiment.

Now, I have heard people say that a sprinter does not push off — he pulls. Well, if he pulls, then he does not need a block because he is not using the back of the block.

A sprinter should have his strongest leg back to initiate the starting movement.

We like to have our sprinters get the feeling of a spring being compressed. A sprinter should want a starting block where his foot can fit snugly. The entire foot should be touching the block, including the heel. From watching films and studying the starting action, I have found that when using a short block and the sprinter's heel extends back over it, if he has been taught to push off the rear block, his heel will go back over the top. Consequently, he will lose one-tenth of a second right there.

If, on the other hand, his foot is solid against a base, then when the gun goes off, his first reaction is to move *out*, since he cannot go backward. He will push off. He has the pressure on the block. Therefore, he will push off with his rear leg.

Ideally, sprinters should be lined up in front of their blocks. All starters should be instructed to say: *Gentlemen, get in front of your blocks. Now take your mark.* Then the athlete would have the opportunity to back into the block, not set on the block, but back into it. After stretching both hamstrings, he should place his front leg in, and then his back leg. He should compress himself back in there and place his hands behind the line. Then he is in his block.

Assuming the initial starting position is similar to putting on a glove, sprinters should work their way into the fingers of the glove. Starting should be done the same way. A sprinter should not have to set on it as many starters instruct our athletes to do. Instead, they should be allowed to get in from the front of the blocks.

A sprinter's feet should not be bent or cramped on the start. They should be snug against the block but the toes should be just touching the ground. If he gets his foot above the ground, he can shoot out a little faster but that is illegal. A good starter will catch this and call a jump against the sprinter. The hands must be behind the line since a sprinter is in violation if he touches any part of the 2-inch line.

Characteristics of an Outstanding Sprinter

* High knee action.
* Powerful long strides.
* Relaxation in the hands, jaw, arms, and shoulders.
* Powerful arm action.
* Forceful, quick sweep back of the leading leg and arm.
* Good elasticity and flexibility in the hips.
* Natural rhythm.
* Good start technique.
* Reaction and reflex time.

16

Set Position. When preparing for the *Set* command, the sprinter should have his body weight comfortably distributed. A balanced start is essential, one which allows him to be leaning forward. If he places too much weight forward on his hands, he will likely be tied up by the time the starter's gun goes off. His shoulders and upper back should be relaxed, not all humped up and tight. I want to see the head just hanging loose.

When he comes up to the set position, the sprinter should keep his head straight and not let it bend up. I like to advise an athlete to think of his body as a straight line, and make sure that his body, neck and torso are all in one straight line.

On the *Set* command, I tell the sprinters to come up quickly but not too fast because they feel as though they are up there forever and have a tendency to roll out or jump. A sprinter should not come up too slowly because he might be left. According to the correct procedure of starting, the starter never fires the gun until every athlete comes up to the set position for at least one second. As a rule, they hold between 1.5 and 2.0, although every once in a while we get a fast gun at about eight-tenths of a second.

On the initial start, the body of the sprinter should have the proper angle so that a straight line can be drawn up from the front block through his legs, hips, torso, neck, and head. If the sprinter's head is bent down and the line goes above it, then he is leaning too much and will lose some of his thrust.

As to the right angle or number of degrees, I believe a coach is wrong to insist that every athlete come up with a certain angle. Every athlete is different and making him conform to a certain angle may tie him up.

At UCLA, we prefer to watch and when we see our sprinters coming out quickly and getting a good transition, we feel that is good for them. Spectators, as a rule, do not know what good transition is. All they see is who gets out of the blocks first.

A serious fault of many sprinters is pulling the foot away from the rear block slightly on the set command which causes the individual to reach back when pushing off. Usually when a sprinter does this, the block was not secure or not firm against his rear foot.

Forming a Tripod with the Hands. For some reason, many of our sprinters today have the wrong hand position at the start. They are placing almost all of their weight on their thumb and forefinger. As a result, they cannot stay up in the set position as long. Their arms start to tighten up and shake, causing jumps.

Our sprinters are instructed to form a tripod and be up on all finger tips. All fingers should be in play, not just the thumb and forefinger. The athletes are encouraged to work on this. Usually their fingers are weak because nothing has been done to strengthen them. It is recommended that sprinters do pushups on their finger tips to strengthen their fingers. I definitely feel they will move out faster if they distribute their weight on all fingers instead of those in front; otherwise, they tighten up too fast

As for breathing, our sprinters are instructed that the moment the starter says *Set*, as they come up, they inhale deeply and hold their breath until the gun goes off. There are coaches who tell their sprinters not to pay any attention to their breathing.

Some athletes like to start with their hips way up, which means the rear leg is straight. Frankly, I do not see how they can get a good push-off because the leg is already straight.

Sprinters are instructed to practice holding their set position for slightly more than two seconds to be sure. The starters are directed by the rules to allow an interval of approximately two seconds, and when all are motionless, discharge the pistol.

Some runners try to anticipate the start by timing the peak of their elevation simultaneously with the gun going off. This is called a rolling start and is an illegal move. Therefore, do not practice it. One false start can disqualify a sprinter from the race.

Starting Action. Just before the gun sounds, we want our sprinters to think movement; in fact, any word that means movement. I want them to be thinking movement so intently that when the gun goes off, they will be moving. Their bodies will react faster to the sound of the gun if their minds are on go-go-go.

The mind has to tell the muscles to react. Experiments have proved that for even the greatest sprinters in the world, it takes from one-tenth to two-tenths of a second from the time the gun goes off. Therefore, if a sprinter is thinking movement, he will have a jump on the opponents because he has the stimulus going.

The athlete should be concentrating not on the bang, but on the very first sound he hears go off. When the gun goes off, he should take off, even if he believes somebody jumped. This is the biggest mistake that our athletes make and one on which may coaches do not work. Sprinters must be trained to drive out of the blocks whether or not they think it is a jump, because many times starters do not call them back. Consequently, they slow down and the race is still going. Suddenly it is necessary for them to pour it on and they cannot run relaxed. Our athletes are told to run all-out every time until they hear that second gun.

While considerable theory and discussion have taken place on how high and far out the sprinter's foot should go, he should only worry about how fast he can go and not raise the foot. He should shoot out as low to the ground as possible.

How far should a sprinter's leg go before it is set down? This is a question athletes continually ask and I simply tell them, *It is up to you. If you stumble, it is one of two things, the rear leg is either too long or two short. You are either stretching out too far with that leg, or you are coming down too soon. The first should be whatever is natural for you. If a sprinter raises his rear leg* up to bring it down, he has lost time. Then he should adjust the length of his step until he can come out smoothly.

If the rear leg comes very low to the ground, shooting out there and coming down, the sprinter is in balance. He does not have to measure to find out how far out the leg is. When shoving off the block, he should be coming out booming.

If a sprinter's right leg is in the rear, I like to get off to the side, then get off to his right, and just watch his rear leg. If he stumbles, the coach has to determine whether he is bringing it out too far or bringing it down too soon.

Since we emphasize bringing the rear leg down fast, he may bring it down too quickly and stumble. Then he does not get the full extension or drive off the front block.

As a sprinter drives off with his rear leg, at the same time, the opposite arm must drive up, so that the upper part of that arm is up around ear level. As a result, his hips are brought down into the position we want.

As the back leg is coming down and the opposite arm is driving up, all of the power comes off the sprinter's front leg. If he executes correctly, he will get full extension off his toes on that front block. Then he will be in good shape with his hips down.

Just before the gun sounds, we want our sprinters to think "movement."

Running Out of the Blocks. The more a coach can emphasize to his sprinters that they get the feeling of running out of the blocks, the faster they are going to become. Even though they will not come on too fast the first time, they will become faster and faster. When athletes think merely of exploding out, they they do not know what to do with their arms, As a result, they have poor transition.

By continuing to accelerate in a smooth motion, a sprinter will eventually attain maximum acceleration. He knows all he has to do is move faster out of the block and not worry about exploding. He is doing everything correctly, and when he gets himself in better shape and learns what he is doing, he is going to be faster out of the blocks.

As he runs out of the blocks, the sprinter's head should still be down, even with his body at a 45° angle. Then his body will straighten up a little bit, and his eyes will be looking more and more down the track. As is done with race horses, some sprinters would benefit through the use of blinders which would prevent them from looking at runners next to them.

Ideally, a sprinter should be trained to look straight ahead. Even at 90 yards, he is generally looking around, trying to use peripheral vision to determine how close the opponents are to him. It should not make a bit of difference if a man is coming up to pass him. The sprinter who tries to do something different and deviates from his relaxed manner of striding will likely tie up and lose out at the tape.

Ideally, a sprinter should be trained to look straight ahead.

Transition Into Running

A key to a good start is for the sprinter to get into running stride as soon as he can. When he has a start so smooth that people can hardly see the transition, he has accomplished something. Getting the proper transition to a running stride, however, is not that easy.

The start of a sprint is like shifting a car from first to second to get into cruising speed. During the first 20 yards, the sprinter is trying to get into that smooth acceleration in which he wants to travel. If he does not do it correctly, the transition from the start to top running form will be jerky.

Warren Edmondson, our 1972 NCAA champion in the 100 meters who was injured in the 200 meter finals, was probably the greatest in knowing how to come out quick and fast. Warren had a tremendous advantage because he was able to make the transition from acceleration to top speed smoothly.

The transition factor is the principal reason we advocate a medium start. Our sprinters appear to have less difficulty in making the transition from acceleration to top running speed smoothly. While the bunch start can provide a powerful thrust, our sprinters have experienced a more difficult transition period when using this type of start. While a sprinter can shoot out and explode impressively on the bunch start, getting the proper transition to his running stride can be difficult.

Therefore, the transition from upward acceleration to a smooth running stride is of major importance. This transition should be so smooth and natural that it is almost unnoticeable.

Through hours and hours of practice, the runner learns how to increase his acceleration until maximum speed is attained without sacrificing relaxation. His basic objective is learning to accelerate and not throw off his body coordination. He must keep his arms and legs synchronized.

Top relaxed speed is the most economical way that a sprinter's body can function. For example, if a sprinter reaches his top speed at approximately 60 yards, but continues to try to accelerate, he will fail to synchronize his arms and legs properly, and will probably tie up at 90 yards. His opponent who reached his top speed at 60 realized he could not go any faster, and just tried to maintain his speed without working any harder. Everything else being equal, he probably won.

In our drills, the sprinters learn to run along very fast, and all of a sudden pick it up and accelerate. With great sprinters, the acceleration or transition from the blocks takes place anywhere from 15 to 25 yards. They literally shoot or run out of the blocks. I prefer to call it running, not exploding, and it is how fast they can run out of the blocks. Actually, with great sprinters, the transition from the start to running form cannot be seen. Their movement out of the lean towards a more upright carriage is gradual. With those who have not mastered this art, there is a little hesitation. This is where the good sprinters shoot out in front, perhaps 3 or 4 yards, which makes the race tough from then on.

Sprinting Action

Sprinting involves the movement of the arms and legs in a coordinated action which takes extensive practice to develop. We work a long time getting
the sprinters' legs and arms coordinated, and synchronizing the arms with
the legs.

Some athletes try hard to use their arms vigorously, but since they are not
synchronized properly with their legs, they tie up quickly. Other runners lift
their knees high and try a quick leg action, without doing anything with their
arms.

If a runner would pump his arms as quickly as possible, he would find that
his legs will usually follow what the arms do. However, he has to start out
slowly and get his arms and legs working together Then, over a period of
weeks and months, gradually he runs faster and faster. He cannot learn how
to relax at a fast pace. This is why we start in the fall and spend four months,
five days a week with the sprinters teaching them how to run properly, what
is relaxed and best for each individual. After the Christmas vacation, we go
into more individual workouts and start preparing them for the outdoor
season.

**Sprinting involves the movement of the arms and legs in a coordinated action which
takes extensive practice to develop.**

The Stride. A smooth, relaxed, and natural stride is beautiful to watch. A full and powerful drive against the ground is essential in an effective stride. Contractions of the extensor muscles of the legs supply a great deal of the forward power which serves as the pushing force that lengthens the stride. A long and powerful leg push drives the body forward.

Sprint speed can be increased either by improving the length of the stride or the rate of striding. However, since the rate of striding is largely determined by individual differences, a great deal of the coaching emphasis is placed on lengthening the stride.

Generally, each sprinter has his or her own most efficient stride length which can be increased by the development of greater muscular strength, elasticity or flexibility, and joint mobility. The thrust of the leg against the ground is responsible for an increase in stride length. A runner is driven forward by the forceful extension of the hip, knee and ankle joint of the leg in contact with the ground, combined with the fast, forceful pull-through of the other recovery leg.

Use an Arm Style Which Feels Relaxing and Comfortable. During our fall program, we have each of our runners experiment and try different arm styles to find out which is best for him. Their knee lift and body lean are checked while they are running at various speeds to see which style is the most efficient and relaxed for them. As a coach, I do not feel I have the right to tell an athlete which one to use. He is the only person who knows which feels the best.

Generally, I have the athlete stand up straight, with his feet together and his arms hanging at his side. Then I ask him to bend his elbows by lifting the lower part of his arms without lifting his shoulders. After holding them there for a while, he is told to begin swinging them back and forth. As a result, he can tell whether or not the arm carry is relaxing or fatiguing. If he wants to do so, he can move them to a lower thrust, whatever feels relaxing to him.

If he sees that a style is definitely hurting the athlete, the coach should tell him. However, he should not always be telling his runners how to run. Leave it up to the athlete but keep reminding him, *Are you relaxed? Does this feel good to you? Do you want to experiment with a higher knee lift? Do you want to use a different arm carry?*

Even though he has considerable knowledge and experience, a coach can make a mistake if he tells every athlete how to run. Much of the time, he should be observing, checking with the athlete, and trying to help him do the correct thing. Let the athlete make most of the suggestions.

Arm Action. While the action of a sprinter's arms must be vigorous and rapid, it must be kept smooth, relaxed, and comfortable. His upper arm and forearm form approximately a right angle. The arms move forward and backward in line with the direction in which the runner is moving. We look for arm action that carries the arms forward and back instead of across the body.

Correct arm action enables the runner to keep his body in proper alignment, preventing it from weaving from side to side. By keeping the trunk of the body steady, maximum power can be applied forward.

Leg speed and arm speed are linked together. The faster the legs go, the faster the arms must move. A sprinter can speed his arm action by assuming the proper angle for him, thus allowing him to pump them as fast as the speed of his legs. The faster the arms are pumped, the faster the legs go.

How he carries his arms will be dependent on his comfort. If he feels tightness coming on, he can make an adjustment by raising or lowering his arm swing.

The backward movement of the arms is as important as the forward thrust— both must be quick and powerful, but never jerky. One of track's most familiar axioms is *The faster the arm action, the faster the legs will go*. To a large degree, this is true. If a runner synchronizes his arms and legs, the faster he moves his arms, his legs should move with them. They work hand in hand.

A Slight Forward Lean Which Is Comfortable. We like our runners to lean a little at the hips, perhaps sacrificing the high knee lift they might have. Otherwise, we do not worry about body lean. A sprinter's body will lean naturally to stay in balance the the amount of lean will depend on his rate of acceleration and air resistance. If he is doing everything right, body lean will take care of itself.

The center of gravity is just a little bit forward and not straight over the plant foot. The result is a pushing, not a pulling action by the legs. In coaching young sprinters, we are constantly observing their center of gravity to determine what position is the most relaxing and comfortable for them.

However, there are some physiologists who believe sprinters run better if they maintain an upright body carriage because it allows the hips to come through and the knees can be lifted higher. Physiologically, they are probably correct, but it is difficult for many athletes to master the upright body carriage. When they begin to tire, they start to go backwards. As a result, their legs become pullers instead of pushers.

Bud Winters had most of his great sprinters, like Tommy Smith and John Carlos, run in the upright position. Some of them were very long-legged athletes and it was easier for them to get the upright position with their long legs.

In my judgement, a comfortable forward lean can help the runner achieve gravity ahead of the striding foot as it contacts the ground.

The key as far as body is concerned is the hips. Hip action must feel loose and relaxed. When the sprinter comes out of the blocks and is trying to drive out, he wants his hips underneath so he can project them forward. Too many try to lean from their hips up; in other words, they are just bending the upper part of their bodies.

If the sprinter has a tendency to straighten up within a few yards of the start, generally, he is not moving fast enough in his opening steps. He should be instructed to try to stay low, drive harder on each step, and lift his knees higher.

Hip Action. The importance of good hip action should receive emphasis in training sprinters. We strive for considerable flexibility in the pelvic region, similar to that of a hurdler. As the knee drives up, the hip should roll forward. The greater the flexibility of the hips, the longer the stride will be. Good explosion of the rear foot and drive up of the knee are partly the result of rolling the hips forward.

Top sprinters have always enjoyed unusually good hip and thigh mobility which enables them to get their knees up and forward easily. Therefore, considerable time must be spent with flexibility and stretching exercises, the type performed regularly by hurdlers. They should be a daily routine.

The most effective way to promote mobility is to encourage knee lifting and hamstring muscle stretching in warm-up calisthenics. If he can raise his knee to his chest without too much effort, surely an athlete will be able to lift it more easily to the proper sprinting height during his stride.

Great sprinters run with high knee action. A high knee lift contributes power and drive. The upper leg is parallel to the ground. It throws the legs out farther and increases the stride. In addition to lengthening the stride, it adds to the force of the pushing leg against the ground. Good action of the knees is the result of foot and ankle explosion off the rear or driving foot. The greater the force in which the lead knee is driven up and out, the greater will be the force in which the rear foot can exert against the ground. However, the runner should be careful not to bring his knees up so high that he is forced to lean backward instead of forward. With high knee action, the speed of the lead foot can be increased significantly. Along with a high knee lift, the foreleg reaches forward as the leg starts down. However, a great deal of practice and training are required.

Great sprinters run with high knee action.

25

Run on the Toes. A sprinter must learn to run on his toes. Many runners have a tendency to run flat-footed. In teaching our sprinters and hurdlers, we use the words *running tall,* which means up on their toes. The runner who runs flat-footed will stay on the ground too long. For speed and power, a sprinter has to keep his body weight forward on the balls of the feet. If his heel hits the ground, he is in real trouble, because it not only slows him down, but jars his entire body.

A good sprinter stays high up on his toes. As a result, his heel will never be seen hitting the ground, I tell our runners, *Why do you run on the back of your foot when there are no spikes there to help you?* We have them work on numerous drill which will help them get up on their toes where they feel as though they are really accelerating.

Most great runners, those who are sprinters and distance runners, run a little pigeon-toed. To the other extreme, some sprinters run with their toes pointed out but they do not run as fast. However, trying to change them will tie them up completely, and it would take years. All a coach does is frustrate them, so I do not try to change them too much. If I see somebody using a duck walk and he is running well, I will not change his style too much.

Relax the Jaw Muscles. By looking at his jaw muscles, I can tell immediately if the athlete's head and neck are relaxed. If his jaw is set, then I know he is tight, and will not run as fast or very far without tying up. Therefore, the main thing that is emphasized to him is that his mouth should be open and his jaw flapping.

If the coach merely says, *Your neck is tight,* or *you are just too rigid up there,* it really does not tell the athlete what to do. He does not know what the coach wants him to do. What the coach should say is: *Just relax your facial muscles and let your jaws bounce.* Immediately, his neck relaxes and he begins to roll his head a bit.

Some people were critical of the way Wayne Collett rolled his head. However, he broke two world records in the intermediate hurdles and the 440. Generally, this is left up to the athlete. All we look at are the facial muscles to see if they are relaxed and the jaw is bouncing around. Then I am not going to worry unless I see his head going back. If his head is going back, the jaw muscles will not be relaxed. Again, the key is, *Relax your jaw,* and this will take care of everything as far as the neck and head are concerned.

Foreleg Extension. The reach of the foreleg is important to good sprinting technique because it increases the stride and is placed in such a position that it can whip downward and backward. When the foreleg makes contact with the ground, it must be moving quickly.

Sprinting action involves two basic cycles —drive and recovery. Recovery involves the action of the leg getting back into position for another stride. As the driving foot leaves the ground, the leg flexes and stays flexed as it reverses direction and moves forward. Flexion causes a speed-up in the recovery of the leg.

Ankle Bounce. The range of his ankle movement and the strength of the lower legs are important to a sprinter. Quite often, the action of the lower legs is given too little emphasis in training.

In achieving a powerful stride, the ankles must flex quickly and fully. The lower legs must contribute more effectively to the sprinting action.

Head and Eyes. Ideally, the sprinter should hold his head level and focus his eyes about 30 yards ahead as he sprints. His head should be in a straight line with the trunk of his body. Wayne Collett, of course, was an exception to this rule.

Breathing is essential in sprinting and should come naturally. The sprinter should breath in and out of both his mouth and nose. How should the sprinter breathe? Many athletes have asked this question, and my answer is quite simple. *Do not think about it. Do not worry about it. The less a sprinter worries about breathing, the better he is going to be. Nature will take care of it.*

The Mental Factor in Running. Our runners are instructed to concentrate on now smooth they can run, not to think about their opponents. Each of our athletes is told, *If he is better, then you are not going to beat him anyway. Why worry about him? But, if he is thinking about you and is running tight, even if he is better than you are, and if you run to the best of your ability and are running relaxed, then you might beat him that day.*

Think fluid, think relaxed, synchronize the arms and legs, think of nothing but how fast, relaxed and how smooth you can run this race. If you do everything right, this opponent is only going to beat you if he is better than you are and is doing things right.

If he worries about his opponent, a sprinter is asking for tension. It is difficult to relax and concentrate on his own best effort if he is thinking about someone else.

The Finish. Through the years, we have see more sprinters lead for 90 yards. Then the field starts to catch them, and they fold completely. When they feel that pressure next to them, they try to change their style. It is essential for a young athlete to learn to run his race and never worry about his opponents.

What happens when a sprinter attempts to change his style? Fundamentally, any alteration of the striding action will interfere with the synchronization of the leg and body movements. This, of course, detracts from the force of the drive leg and reduces the speed at the finish.

We have read numerous articles which suggested that coaches teach their sprinters during the last 5 to 10 yards to gather and put on a burst of speed. Let us say, on the 100-yard dash, a sprinter is already going as fast as his body can go. How can he gather additional speed and power suddenly and put on a burst? In doing so, he will likely destroy his concentration, relaxation, and his running style. Since fatigue is starting to set in, all the burst does is bring on fatigue a little faster. By changing his style the last 5 to 10 yards, that athlete will usually lose the race if it is a close one.

Spectators, athletes and coaches can remember seeing a race where every sprinter was coming down almost neck to neck and suddenly, the last 5 yards, the athlete surged ahead. Actually, it was not the finish of that athlete, he simply learned to control his body, and since he did not feel the pressure of the athletes next to him, he sprinted through the finish. As for his opponents, they tried something different and tied up. While to the crowd, it might have looked as though the winner put on a burst of speed, what happened was that the others tied up. No sprinter can put on a burst when he is going as fast as he can.

Warren Edmonson really could run through that tape. He won the 100 meter NCAA championship in 1972 and the NCAA meet record of 10.0. If he had not been injured, he would have proved just how good he was in the 1972 Olympics.

Most of our sprinters have been great at running through the tape. They did not do anything fancy at the tape because we emphasize running 10 yards beyond the finish. If the athlete is going to run 10 yards beyond the finish, he cannot put on any kind of a lunge, shoulder dip or burst at the tape.

Generally, there are three types of finishes— body lunge, forward shrug, and running through or the straight ahead.

★ **Body Lunge.** At the last moment, the runner shoots ahead on his leg that is planted on the ground. However, if he does it too soon, he will likely miss the tape, fall short, and somebody will likely nip him at the tape.

★ **Forward Shrug.** This finish has won many Olympic titles but veteran athletes are necessary to perform the difficult technique. Basically, the sprinter twists, leans, drops the nearest shoulder, and hits the tape ahead of his opponent. The old rule stated that a runner could break the finish plane with his neck, but now it must be with his torso which does not include the neck.

Many of our young athletes try to copy some of the older veterans who have been around a long time and have had the time and experience to develop these gimmicks which must be timed perfectly. But these veterans know everything about their bodies, their movements, and they know what they can do. The novice who tries to copy a great athlete is just going to hurt himself and not win as many races because he lacks the concentration and the know-how in driving through.

If the athlete wants to lean at the finish, he can lean forward from the waist on the last step before the finish line. But he should not let it slow him down, or his finish may lose more races for him than it wins.

★ **Running Through or the Straight Ahead.** We will favor the type of finish in which the athlete sprints through the tape, unless he knows exactly how to time his body lean, body shrug or the lunge. The majority of sprinters perform the more difficult moves wrong. They may have the wrong foot, the improper time or they are not quite close enough to the finish tape and it can cost them the race.

Our athletes are instructed: *If you are running properly, I want you to sprint through the tape*. Novice or inexperienced athletes should be taught how to run through the tape. I have seen more sprinters nipped at the tape because they tried something fancy at the finish. Therefore, our sprinters are urged to go through that tape as though they have another 10 yards to go. We have seen some of our athletes forget what we told them and in lunging at the tape, they fell flat on their faces while the opponent went through.

Another error sprinters make at the finish is the unconscious slowing up at the sight of the approaching string. Or the moment they feel the pressure of an athlete pulling alongside them, they try to get a peek at him which immediately destroys their concentration on what they are trying to do.

Sprinting Strategy. While speed and training are necessary, the sprinter should be an intelligent runner. If two athletes are equal in ability and physical attributes, the one who knows how to take advantage of every situation will reach the finish line first. Above all, a sprinter should always run his own race. Complete concentration is needed. A sprinter must prepare thoroughly for every race. He must work on his conditioning, technique, and attitude.

Who will be the starter? Does he have a fast gun or does he hold the runners in the set position? Does he give all the runners time to settle into the blocks after telling them to take their marks? If he is a fast gun, meaning he starts the race shortly after the *Set* command, be ready.

A sprinter should inspect the track before the race. He should know his lane, He might walk the entire distance in his lane and inspect the surface.

To avoid having to make last-minute adjustments, he should carry his own starting blocks. He must make sure the blocks are working correctly before his race and know the proper adjustment.

Check Out Your Lane. An athlete should always check his lane out the entire distance. There is always the possibility of a hole in the lane or there might be a soft or wet spot and he might slip.

We tell our athletes, *Do not try to run right on that line*. If they hit that metal or concrete curve, they can be injured. If they hit the white line three consecutive steps and are caught, they are disqualified. It is best to run about 8 inches out, in case the sprinter staggers when he tires, and loses his balance. He should make sure he does not hit the line.

A sprinter should learn from every race. After it is over, he, along with his coach, must analyze what he did— what he did right and the things he did wrong. This analysis will aid him considerably in planning future practices to overcome weaknesses so he can do better next time.

2

JIM HINES
GOLD MEDAL WINNER

Stanley V. Wright,
Western Illinois University

Illustrations 1 through 12, Series A, show the first quarter final heat of the 100 meters in Mexico City. In the second race of the day for the sprinters, Jim Hines was in lane 5; Enrique Figuerola, Cuba in lane 4; and Lennox Miller, Jamaica in lane 6. We had been concerned about Jim's start, because prior to going to Lake Tahoe in August he had trouble with mechanics and concentration. However, during his stay in Tahoe and through Mexico City he did not have a false start.

It might be interesting to mention that the Mexican sprinter who started all eight heats of the first round in the morning did not start any of the races in the quarter-finals that afternoon. This had an effect on Jim because the starter in the morning was 0.1 to 0.3 seconds slower than the starter in the afternoon.

Since Jim was in the first heat in the quarter-finals, he did not have an opportunity to make the adjustment to the cadence of the afternoon starter. After the race, we both agreed that he had not been ready at the start and he had to give his next two races a little more concentration on the start and mechanics of getting off the blocks. Despite a poor start in this race, Jim ran 10.1 and finished second to Lennox Miller's 10.1 and Figuerola's third in 10.2.

Illustrations 1 through 10, Series B, show Jim Hines running the first heat of the 100 meters in the National AAU meet in Sacramento. In this heat Jim ran a 9.8 100 meters with a 6.2 aiding wind. The runners in the illustrations are Ronnie Smith in lane 8 who was second in 10.0 and Kirk Clayton in lane 6 who was third in 10.0.

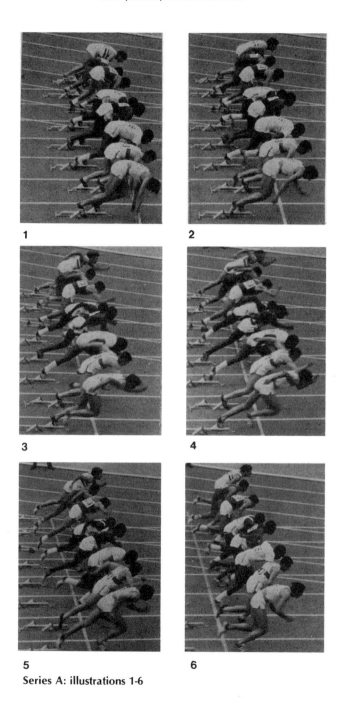

1

2

3

4

5

6

Series A: illustrations 1-6

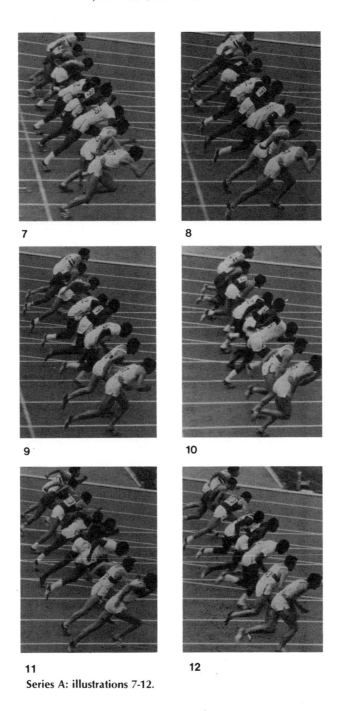

7   8

9   10

11   12
Series A: illustrations 7-12.

We are not certain at what distance the runners are, but they are fairly close to the finish line (about 5 to 10 meters).

Illustration A1 shows that Jim was never in the proper set position on the blocks. His center of gravity is too low and his hips and shoulders are in a poor position to facilitate his starting action.

As shown in Illustration A2, Jim's arm action is poor basically because his weight is not properly distributed through his arms and shoulder girdle in the set position. Therefore, he was not able to attain maximum velocity off the starting blocks and his rear leg snapped through with little force.

Mainly due to poor arm action Jim has started to overstride and his overstriding has straightened his body angle too soon placing him in an upright position less than two strides off the blocks (Illustrations A3 and A4).

It appears to us that Jim may be in a chopping motion (Illustrations A5 and A6). This improper motion came about because of his poor body angle and lack of power. He had to chop to regain his balance and rhythm which put him slightly behind some of the runners in the heat at the first five meters.

Illustrations A7, A8, and A9 show that Jim's body angle is too close to the vertical when he is not more than three full strides off the blocks. At three strides he is almost running his normal body angle which he generally does not reach until he is 20 to 25 yards off the blocks.

As shown in Illustrations A10, A11, and A12, Jim is still trying hard to get his body under good control and balance in preparation for the sprinting action. With a good start, he would generally reach his maximum velocity approximately 7 to 8 seconds after leaving the blocks. Because of his poor start, he was not able to obtain his maximum velocity and was defeated in the heat by Lennox Miller.

As shown in these illustrations, Jim has started to accelerate towards the finish line. His body angle is good and he is running with good balance and rhythm. Illustrations B1 and B2 show Jim landing on the toes of his left foot in preparation for the pushing action, and in Illustrations B2 and B3 his right knee is high with the thigh forming a right angle to his body. The high knee lift also gives him time for the pushing foot to gain full extension (Illustrations B4, B5, and B6) and time for this leg to lessen the angle it makes with the ground (Illustrations B5, B6, and B7).

Jim's toes are pointed straight ahead, because toeing-in or toeing-out would cause lateral sway and would also shorten his stride. In all of the illustrations, his leg actions comes through in the same plane which directs his balance and rhythm in a straight line.

As shown, Jim's arms are carried close to the side of his body which prevents a shoulder roll. His arms also swing forward until the hands reach shoulder level (Illustration B3). Jim's emphasis on arm movement is forward and backward; if the pictures showed a front view, it would perhaps be noticed that his arms swing across the body until the hands meet the mid-sagittal plane of the body.

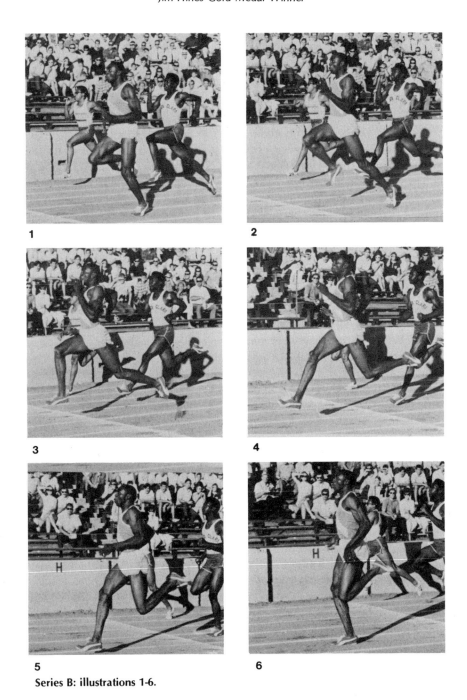

1 **2**

3 **4**

5 **6**

Series B: illustrations 1-6.

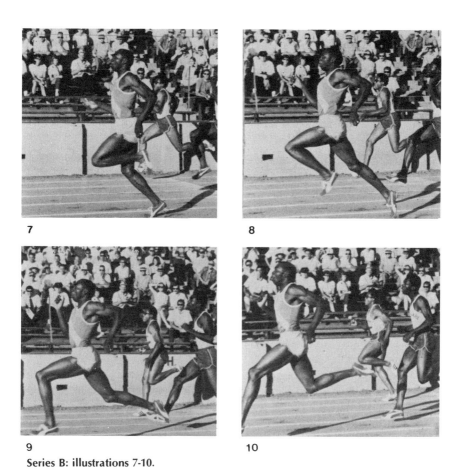

7   8

9   10
Series B: illustrations 7-10.

As Jim nears the finish line, he increases his speed by increasing the length of his strides rather than increasing the number of strides. Many sprinters still make the mistake of increasing the number of strides near the finish line. In all of the illustrations, his head is carried on a level with his eyes focused on a line that falls below the horizontal.

3

COACHING THE SPRINT START

G. G. Dales,
Western Michigan University

Coaching the sprint start begins with a realization of the importance of this phase of the sprint race. Time and study must be given to a few preliminary considerations:

● Good starting technique often decides a sprint race.

● Individual differences in anatomical structure and body mechanics must be considered in arriving at optimum block setting, hip height, forward lean, and length of the first few strides. Owens, Morrow, Sime, and Murchison all differed in starting techniques to some degree. For an·individual to attempt to follow a style which is not suited to him may prove unsuccessful.

● For the best results complete relaxation, poise, and concentration are most desirable qualities. They must be practiced along with the body movements in taking the marks, getting set, and in exploding off the blocks.

Well-coached sprinters do not jump the gun. Coaching the start should include practice in developing confidence, control, and discipline. A sprinter should develop confidence in his ability to move with the sound of the gun, and control and discipline to keep from jumping the gun when it is held two or more seconds as specified in the rules.

● Once a sprinter gains an advantage of a few inches over his opponents at the start, he needs to run only as fast as the others to win. A sprinter who finds himself in this desirable situation must practice running at top speed and remain relaxed to stay ahead of his opponents.

● Good starting technique is but one phase of the sprint race which requires coaching and practice. However good the start, it is·of little or no advantage unless the pick-up, the body of the race and the finish are conscientiously coached and practiced.

After each of the points is recognized and comprehended, then the actual coaching of the mechanics of the sprint start can begin.

Setting the Starting Blocks

Considerable experimentation may be necessary to assist the sprinter in finding his most efficient foot, arm, body, and head position at the start. In order to assume a comfortable set position without crowding or settling back, the sprinter can begin by setting the blocks at their maximum distance. The starting line is not needed in these early stages; in fact, it can be an undesirable influence. The hands and the rear block can be adjusted so that the distance between the blocks, permit balance and maximum potential forward thrust from the set position.

Taking the Marks

Beginners may be uncertain about which foot to place on the front block. This predicament can be solved by asking the runner to go through a pantomime of a football punt or a conventional high jump. The drive or take-off foot (not the kicking foot) is in most cases the foot which will be most effective on the front block.

The blocks should be set and tried, and the sprinter should be ready when the starter calls the runners to their marks. At the command, the sprinter assumes a relaxed five-point position by kneeling on the knee of his back leg. His knees should be directly in line, the balls of his feet should be placed solidly against the blocks, and his toes should just touch the ground. Relaxation can be practiced at this point by shaking the hands and wrists just before placing them behind the starting line. A bridge should be formed between the thumb and the fingers as the hands are placed parallel to the line. The arms should be straight to form a solid support for the body. In this position concentration on the starter's commands and upon control and relaxation are most important. Dropping the head and keeping the jaw, neck, and shoulder muscles loose will help to eliminate all stimuli but the sound of the gun.

Getting Set

At the command *get set*, the sprinter raises his knees and hips as he leans slightly forward to assume a four-point position of balance and poise between his feet which are against the blocks and his hands which are on the ground. His hips should come up to at least shoulder height if not slightly higher, and his arms should be brought to vertical or slightly more forward of vertical at the shoulders. Periodically, the coach and the sprinter should review certain check points:

● Check the sprinter's foot alignment on the blocks. The heels and the balls of the feet should be straight up and down, and the toes should just touch the ground.

● Check the straight-forward alignment of his body. The knees should be directly in front of the feet on the blocks, and the arms should be in line with the shoulders.

● Check the angle between the lower leg and thigh of his front leg. More or less than 90 degrees will permit less than maximum forward drive.

● Check the position of the sprinter's arms. If they are unsteady or if they bend at the elbows, the forward lean may be too great. The starting blocks may need to be moved back a few inches to permit a more forward position of the hands. For the sprinter who might still have difficulty in supporting his weight, it may help him to lock his elbows (not stiff) and to rotate them toward his chest.

● Check the shoulder and neck muscles for absence of tension. Notice the difference in tension in Illustrations A1 and A2.

● Check the sprinter's breathing habits. See that he inhales as he moves into the set position. Then he should exhale a little and hold his breath until the gun is fired or until the starter calls him up.

Murchison's powerful arms permit him to exaggerate the forward lean (illustration A1). This gives him the feeling of being ahead even before the race begins. With his controversial straight but relaxed back leg barely in contact with the rear block, he has eliminated one motion in the movement of his leg, that of straightening a conventional bent back leg before bending it again as some sprinters do. Murchison merely rests his back leg on the block and he is able to bring it up more quickly to a bent position at the stimulus from the sound of the gun. He feels he can combine the *drive-off* from the front block by the strong front leg with the *running-out* of the block by the relaxed back leg. Notice the difference in the contracted and relaxed calf muscles in Illustrations A1 and A2. Furthermore, he has an advantage in being able to assume the same leg and hip position at the set position before each start.

At the Gun

At the crack of the gun we can clearly observe how and why Murchison has been labeled the fastest starter in the world. He achieves maximum forward thrust with the drive from his front foot. His hand and arm on the side of his front foot swing forward and up while the opposite upper arm and elbow swing back to a point where they are visible from his back (Illustration A3). His back is straightened forward as it continues parallel to the ground.

The knee of his back leg reaches forward and up until his thigh is at least at a right angle to his upper body, while the drive leg on the front block has reached maximum extension (Illustration A4). A straight line can be extended from the front block through the ball of his foot, ankle, knee, hip, shoulder, and head. The relaxed opposite leg has come up from the rear

Illustrations 1-6. These photos show Ira Murchinson as the lead-off man for Western Michigan's sprint relay team in the 1958 Drake Relays.

block and it drops just ahead of the starting line where it now becomes the front and driving leg. It in turn drives forward to maximum extension as if it were driving from a front starting block. Again, a straight line can be extended from the ground through the body as before. We superimposed the negative from Illustration A4 on Illustration A6, and found no visible increase in body angle although Murchison's legs and arms have alternated positions a full stride. The only observable change is a slight rise in the focus of his eyes a bit farther down the track toward the finish line. Murchison's ability to maintain his lean in the early stages of the sprint and his ability to combine this with a high knee lift gives him a powerful thrust with each stride.

In conclusion, sprinters can be coached to good starts with intensive practice at least three days a week using a gun, but only after a thorough warm-up. Before any serious running, Murchison warms up for 45 minutes to an hour. His practice schedule includes starts three times a week after four to five weeks of preliminary conditioning in the form of stretching and bounding exercises as well as jogging, striding, and overdistance running interspersed with short bursts of sprinting. Starts are practiced following one-half of the planned workout for the day. We begin with four to six starts on Tuesdays early in the indoor season in December. Murchison builds up to 15 or 20 starts on Thursdays through March. In April we begin to work outdoors when the weather permits. All starts after the first two or three are competitive, and they are run at full effort through 50 or more yards. Following the practice session on starts, the second half of the planned workout for the day is completed.

4

THE CLASSIC 440

Jim Bush,
University of California/Los Angeles

John Smith is great for many reasons, and in many respects just the opposite of Wayne Collett, who is equally great. John is 6 feet, 2 inches tall and weighs between 180 and 190 pounds, depending on the time of the season. His best running weight is about 185 pounds. John is strong and loose. He is becoming stronger all the time, with a noticeable increase in speed each year. An example is the 9.4 hundred he ran in Miami, Florida right after the Pan-American Games, in an AAU meet, into a 5 mile per hour wind. His last timed 100-yard dash was his freshman year in an allcomers meet during the summer, in 9.7 seconds. His 220 time has also come down from 21.8 to 20.6. This has been accomplished with very little speed work, which backs up our theory that strength, endurance, pace, and relaxation, with very little speed work will still bring out the speed if the man has any to bring out.

The real key to John is his ability to relax while running at a very fast pace. This is something we work on constantly.

Because we have worked on strength, pace, running curves, relaxation, etc., John has been able to bring his time down from 47.5 as a high school senior to 44.5 in a period of just three years. We might add, he ran the greatest paced-relaxed 440 ever. The splits were 22.2 for the first 220 and 22.3 for the second 220. What was significant, however, was the way he and Wayne finished the race. Both were still relaxed, knees high, with good form as they ran through the tape. The balance of the field was tied up as they finished. We honestly believe that both John and Wayne would have run closer to 44.0 if they had been next to each other, instead of five lanes apart. They still had run left and would have pushed each other to faster times.

John Smith

Wayne Collett on the outside.

However, one runner breaking the world record and the other tying the old world record, with their first and second placing from the same school, is not bad.

First of all, let us explain the style Wayne Collett uses. He is strong and powerful, and was faster at an earlier age than John. Wayne ran 9.5 and 47.1 in high school. As a freshman, he ran 20.2 and 44.9 for the 200 and 400 meters, both national freshman records. As a sophomore, Wayne ran 9.4 without any real speed work. He had the speed to run 9.1 or 9.2 if we had wanted to work him as a pure sprinter.

Wayne has a unique style of running, which many people criticize. He runs with his head rolling from side to side, mouth open, hands open, with the wrists relaxed, letting the hands flop up and down. This does have a tendency to make Wayne wobble within his lane, but, most important, he runs relaxed and this is his way of running relaxed. Had we insisted on changing his style, we probably would have tied him up in knots. Wayne's 47.1 to 44.7 is enough proof, as far as we are concerned, of his sound running style.

As can be seen, Wayne and John have a great deal in common in many respects, and achieve the same end results, but are at almost exact opposite ends as far as running style or form is concerned. Both stand 6 feet, 2 inches tall and weigh about 185 pounds. Both have run 9.4 for the 100-yard dash without working a great deal on speed and both are not far apart in their 220 and 440 times. Both men are powerful, and have tremendous acceleration. Wayne has more explosiveness, where John is smoother and can overcome another man's explosive start. John runs out of the blocks. Wayne can, when he concentrates, explode out of the blocks.

In their classic world record 440-yard race, Wayne ran 21.3 at the 220 mark, and John ran 22.2. In all fairness, Wayne was in lane seven, and John was in lane two. John knew where Wayne was all the time, and Wayne had no way of knowing where John was until he caught him with 50 yards to go.

They should both hit the 220 in about 21.9 and carry it in from there if they want to reach their full potential, and lower the world record down where we feel they can place it.

The 440-yard run must be considered a 440-yard dash. Research has shown that a man cannot build up any more speed somewhere past the 60-yard mark if he is going all out. Even a sprinter cannot continue to build, or go faster in a 100-yard dash after 60 yards. How can a man run a 440-yard dash and not tie up? It does not matter whether a coach is working with a world class athlete or an average runner (around 48 seconds), the same philosophy should be used.

A runner should not worry about his opponent. He should run his own race at all times, and if he is the better man, he will win, providing he has trained properly.

How should an athlete be trained so he will be able to run 440 yards at a tremendous pace, and finish without tying up in knots? Drills should be used to learn how to run into the curve, off the curve, how to hold a relaxed-fast pace, how to build on the home stretch, and still remain relaxed. This is not an easy task. Overdistance drills are needed, and speed drills with pace and relaxation should be emphasized constantly.

In order to run the 440-yard dash correctly, the runner must come out of the blocks as would a sprinter, sprint the first curve fast, come off the curve with considerable speed, hold that speed with a relaxed pace, without slowing down, and then start building as he enters the second curve, still remaining relaxed. As he comes off the second curve, he should start to build slowly and continue this right through the tape trying to maintain a relaxed, but fast pace. If the athlete has learned all of these techniques, then he should try to run the first 220 one to two tenths faster than his second 220.

Too much emphasis is placed on what lane a man is in. A sprinter should learn to run in all lanes, always run his race, and make his opponent adjust to him. Naturally, the inside lanes have sharper curves and are harder to run, but the runner can also see all the other runners. The outside lanes are easier to run, but the runner does not know where his opponents are. The middle lanes are the best because the entire field can be seen pretty well and the athlete knows what is going on at all times.

5

ARM ACTION IN THE 440

Tom Ecker,
Cedar Rapids, Iowa, Community Schools

One of the most important physical functions of a quarter-miler, and often the most neglected, is arm action. Many coaches tend to undervalue arm action in the 440 when a boy can become an improved runner through the proper use of his arms.

Because so much energy is used in so short a time, the 440 has long been regarded as the most grueling event in track and field. A quarter-miler who expends enough energy to be in a good position at the 330 mark often does not have the needed drive to finish with a kick that is comparable to the first three-quarters of his race. For this reason we began experimenting with ways of maintaining good quarter-mile speed throughout the 440 through use of the arms.

Our 440 men use three distinct styles of arm action every time they run a race. From the time the race starts until they reach their quarter-mile pace, they use their arms like sprinters. Then they change to a style that we call form running, which is maintained throughout the greater part of the race. Finally, they finish the race by greatly exaggerating the swing of their arms in the final drive to the finish line.

The Start

At the sound of the gun, the quarter-miler digs out of the blocks similar to a sprinter for the first 30 yards. This opening sprint builds up his energy so that he can maintain near top speed throughout the race.

Many coaches are rather reluctant about having their 440 men come out of the blocks at top speed, because they feel that a boy will use some of the physical strength needed later in the race. Actually, we have found that nervous energy which is stored up for the start carries the runner through the opening drive with little if any loss of physical strength.

Because so much energy is used in so short a time, the 440 has long been regarded as the most grueling event in track and field.

Form Running

After 30 yards, the runner changes to what we call form running. This type of running sustains the speed that the runner has built up coming out of the blocks without using nearly as much energy. The steps are short and rapid about 22 per 50 yards. A runner's arms are not just swung, but are bounced with each step so that his upper arms and shoulders are actually massaged and kept loose.

When running the curves, the form remains the same except that the action of the right arm and leg is a bit more pronounced. The right arm is swung across the chest and toward the pole, while the right leg is driving a little harder than the left. This motion helps the runner keep his balance while rounding the curves.

The Finish

When the runner begins to tire because of the fast pace he has set for himself, he begins to exaggerate his arm action by swinging his fists up to a point in front of his eyes, very much as though he were hitting someone in the jaw. This action prevents his arms and shoulders from tying up in the final run for the tape. While exaggerating the arm swing, he also lifts his knees similar to a sprinter, picking them up and putting them down as rapidly as he is able. To make sure he never slows down at the tape, he continues his drive to a point five yards past the finish line.

Butch Kincaid, one of our sprinters, wanted to be a quarter-miler, but was just not able to run fast enough at the distance. After his first year, Kincaid's best time for the 440 was 53.7. We worked with him for just a week, showing him the arm action methods that are explained. During the next season he ran 50.2, an improvement of three and a half full seconds over his previous best. High school coaches in this area who are teaching the importance of arm action are getting similar results.

We began experimenting with different styles of arm action in an attempt to discover ways of maintaining good quarter-mile speed throughout the 440. The results have shown us just how important his arms are to the quarter-miler. The legs may be the wheel that get the runner to the finish line, but the arms are largely responsible for making those wheels churn.

6

AN OVERDISTANCE TRAINING PROGRAM FOR SPRINTERS

George R. Colfer,
St. Bonaventure University

One of the major problems faced by many high school and some college coaches is not having an indoor season, thus making it necessary to prepare their athletes for the outdoor season in a short period of time. In addition, there are delays in training caused by restrictions on the date for starting practice in some areas, athletes involved in other sports, weather conditions, and the use of facilities. Regardless of the time factor, we all must work to get our athletes into the best possible condition in the time that is available.

In referring to sprint men, runners in distances up to and including the 440 and all hurdle events are placed in this category. Overdistance training is not new, but in the past many coaches hesitated to use it for their sprint men. Today some coaches use controlled distance running to increase speed in the off-season.

The training is divided into three phases: 1) the pre-season; 2) in-season; and 3) the competitive season.

Pre-season workouts should begin at least eight weeks before the competitive season starts. This phase could also be termed informal as the practices do not have to be supervised at all times. The workouts are given to the athletes and they complete them mainly on their own. We do not say that the coach should not be present, but it is not mandatory at all times. This is an excellent time for him to teach and work with individuals in perfecting starts, relay exchanges, running and hurdle form or to work with the field events. By having the runners mainly responsible for the pre-season workout, the coach can be free to cover many specifics. This type of practice can also be a bonus to the track coach who possibly has another coaching assignment and wants to get his team started on training.

This pre-season phase last four weeks and is broken into four workouts — one for each week. In our situation, this usually means indoor work because our winters are quite severe. At the end of this four-week period, the goal is to have the athletes conditioned well enough so when the more strenuous work in phase 2 is started, the runners will be able to push themselves into competitive condition with less chance of injury and without overtiring to the point of complete fatigue.

The following workouts for phase 1 are given by events. It is recommended that if a coach has runners in multiple events, they use the pre-season workout for the longest event in which they participate.

Pre-Season Workouts (100-220-440 Relay-800 120HH-180LH-220LH)

First Week. A. Run at one-half speed for 15 minutes - 4 days (Monday, Tuesday, Thursday, and Friday). B. Practice starting form for 15 minutes - 4 days. C. Strength building program - 3 days (Monday, Wednesday, and Friday).

Second Week. A. Run at one-half speed for 20 minutes - 5 days (Monday, through Friday). B. Practice starting form for 15 minutes - 5 days. C. Stride 220, jog 220, two repetitions - 5 days. D. Strength building program - 3 days (Monday, Wednesday, and Friday).

Third Week. A. Run at one-half speed for 25 minutes - 5 days (Monday through Friday). B. Practice starting form for 15 minutes - 5 days. C. Start and stride at three-quarters speed for 50 yards, five repetitions -5 days. D. Stride 220, jog 220, three repetitions - 5 days. E. Strength building program - 3 days (Monday, Wednesday, and Friday).

Fourth Week. A. Run at one-half speed for 30 minutes - 5 days (Monday, through Friday). B. Practice starting form for 15 minutes - 5 days. C. Start and stride at three-quarters speed for 50 yards, five repetitions - 5 days. D. Stride 220, jog 220, four repetitions - 5 days. E. Strength building program - 3 days (Monday, Wednesday, and Friday).

Hurdlers. Add 15 minutes of form work on the hurdles for each running day, and for the third and fourth weeks, the start and sprint will include three flights of hurdles.

Relays. Run two workouts per week carrying the baton. For exchange practice this early in the season, the coach should supervise the work so bad habits are not formed.

Pre-Season Workouts (440-440IH-Mile Relay)

First Week. A. Run at one-half speed for 15 minutes - 4 days (Monday, Tuesday, Thursday, and Friday). B. Practice starting form for 10 minutes - 4 days. C. Stride 220, jog 220, two repetitions - 4 days. D. Strength building program - 3 days (Monday, Wednesday, and Friday).

Second Week. A. Run at one-half speed for 20 minutes - 5 days (Monday through Friday). B. Practice starting form for 10 minutes - 5 days. C. Stride 220, jog 220, three repetitions - 5 days. D. Strength building program - 3 days (Monday, Wednesday, and Friday).

Third Week. A. Run at one-half speed for 25 minutes - 5 days (Monday through Friday). B. Practice starting form for 10 minutes - 5 days. C. Stride 220, jog 220, four repetitions - 5 days. D. Acceleration run for 220, walk 220, two repetitions - 5 days. E. Strength building program - 3 days (Monday, Wednesday, and Friday).

Fourth Week. A. Run at one-half speed for 30 minutes - 5 days (Monday through Friday). B. Practice starting form for 10 minutes - 5 days. C. Stride 220, jog 220, four repetitions - 5 days. D. Acceleration run for 220, walk 220, four repetitions - 5 days. E. Strength building program - 3 days (Monday, Wednesday, and Friday).

Hurdlers. Add 15 minutes of form work on the hurdles for each running day.

Relays Run two workouts per week carrying the baton. For exchange practice this early in the season, the coach should supervise the work so bad habits will not be developed.

Controlled distance running is a technique which can be used to increase speed in the off-season.

Acceleration Run. Begin at a stride and increase gradually in speed throughout distance, never attaining full speed or an all-out sprint, but never decrease speed or slow down the pace.

At the conclusion of these four weeks, if an athlete works conscientiously on his schedule, he should have increased his endurance, leg strength, leg power, and overall body conditioning. At this point he should be ready to drive himself into competitive condition. Any of the schedules can be modified to meet the needs. However, at this point, may we emphasize the principle of overdistance as the standard for increasing endurance, strength, and body condition. It is doubtful that without the distance training for these four weeks an athlete will be ready to move on to the regular or in-season training and perform up to his expectations.

For phase 2 or the in-season practice we are not going to give specific daily workouts because these should be constructed daily to fit the needs of the athletes. Our practice schedules are made up each morning based on the previous days workout and results, the appraisal of the athlete's condition, and in accordance with our coming schedule. Bassically, the following components make up the workouts, not necessarily always in the same order. 1. Warm-up. 2. Pace work. 3. Distance work. 4. Speed work. 5. Specialties (starts, exchanges, form work, etc.). 6. Strength building program.

To incorporate these components into each practice is the coaches' job. In addition, the following list contains certain guidelines for making up these practice schedules that should be followed to assure a quality practice demanding enough to get the athletes into peak condition. This list is based on six practice days per week.

● *Distance running should be continued three times per week.* This can be done at the beginning of practice or at the conclusion of the balance of the workout. Three to five miles are recommended at one-half speed pace.

● *One practice per week should be moved up.* The sprint men should train at the 440 workout level and the 440 runners should train at the 880 workout level.

● *Starts should be practiced at full speed.* We have starting practice daily 30 minutes before the regular workout begins. Thus, the runners work on their specialty when they are fresh and interested and it does away with extending practice.

● *Pace and speed work should be emphasized.* The use of interval training can accomplish this best. Intervals of rest at this phase of practice should be reduced as quickly as possible.

● *The use of overdistance intervals.* As an example, a 440 pace workout may consist of 330 - four repetitions - with three minute intervals followed by an overdistance interval of 660 or 880. The runner should be instructed to push to his limit on this run because it is included for conditioning purposes. Workouts can also be planned using only overdistance intervals for the pace work.

● *Weekly time trials are beneficial to check the progress of the runners.*
The overdistance principle can be of help by extending or lengthening
time trials to fit meet situations. For instance, if a runner is in more than one
event, run him in trials for each event and in the same order as the meet
goes. Another method is on occasion to run the athletes in trials over their
meet distance (give the 440 runners trials in a 600 or 800). Back-to-back time
trials can enhance conditioning and also build an athlete's confidence and
morale. As an example, run a 440 trial, set a rest interval, repeat the trial, and
see if the athlete can maintain the time of his first trial. This is also an excellent way to determine recuperation time needed for those runners who
compete in more than one event or who must run trial heats.

The· competitive season practice (phase 3) has to be worked completely
around the meet schedule. We tend to work lightly on a day prior to a meet
and only work moderately the day after competition, which usually consists
of distance work. Once our season opens, we generally run competitively
twice weekly which narrows down our strenuous practices. However, we
follow the previously mentioned principles and components of in-season
training except on those days prior to or following a meet as explained
previously. Due to the fact that our meet season is strenuous and tiring, we
rely heavily on lasting conditioning effects of the overdistance method for
training our sprint men and hurdlers.

It is a myth that sprinters, etc. cannot endure strenuous training methods.
Inherent speed and natural talents have caused some sprint men to take
workouts lightly and still be successful. However, for the most part there is
no substitute for hard work and training on the part of any runner including
sprinters and hurdlers. A coach should have no regret or hesitation in planning an overdistance training program if it fits his needs.

7

COACHING THE QUARTER-MILERS

Gene Clohecy,
Argentine High School, Kansas City, Kansas

Enumerating the different methods to use in coaching quartermilers would be quite lengthy; however, there is one word which is the key to success, work. Many systems have been used, but all of the effective systems employ work as the theme.

Gone are the days in major competition when a sprinter could take it easy for 300 yards and sprint the last 110 yards. Although many coaches like to employ this method, it is not being used by today's better quarter-milers. At the present time, quarter-milers are sprinting at almost top effort for the 330 yards, staying as relaxed as possible, and calling on their endurance to maintain most of the speed for the last 110 yards. This endurance is not God-gifted as sprinting ability is, but must be built through overdistance.

We have used this idea in our quarter-mile training, and it has resulted in the success of one boy, Drue Jennings. He was the state 440-yard champion as a junior, with times in the state meet of 49.2 and 49.4. As a senior, he set the regional record of 48.3 which is an all-time state best for a boy in high school competition. He set the state record the next week at 48.4. Although this time ranked him only eleventh in the nation, it is noteworthy in Kansas. There were no others of his caliber in the area. Only two other records below 49.0 had been posted in Kansas before Drue's time. Both of these boys were capable of 9.8 or 9.9 consistently in the 100-yard dash. Jennings had a best 100 time of 10.0 and was consistent at 10.2.

Our quarter-mile training consists of overdistance early in the week, and then as the week progresses, working gradually down to speed work. Overdistance consists only of 660's at best effort. Each time a 660 is run, an attempt is made to surpass the best time run earlier. A runner never sprints in practice (for top effort) but tries to sprint at near top effort and maintain relaxation.

Each of our sprinters is given a table, similar to the one shown, early in the season, and is asked to find himself in the sprint column. He looks across the horizontal line to the left to the 440 time on that line. This indicates the 440 of which he is capable. In almost all cases, the sprint speed is better than the indicated time for the 440. The sprinter is told his job is to work on over-distance to bring his endurance time down to the line of his sprint speed. Sprint speed will change, but it does not change drastically in a mature boy. Of course, each boy is encouraged to improve his sprint speed.

Many high school boys have average sprint speed, ranging in the 100 from 10.5 to 10.8. Even these boys can develop themselves into above average quarter-milers. Certainly they are capable of filling a spot on a relay team. Each boy is encouraged not only to drive his endurance time down to the horizontal line of his sprint speed, but beyond. By doing so, he will be able to maintain a near top effort longer and thus reduce his time.

440-Yard Race Planning

If a sprinter wants to run this 440 time, then he must be able to run the following times in practice. The opposite also applies.

	660	330	220	100
58	1:36	43	27	11.2
56	1:33	41	26	11.0
54	1:30	39	25	10.8
52	1:27	37.5	24	10.6
51	1:25.5	37	23.5	10.5
50	1:24.0	36	23.0	10.4
49	1:22.5	35.3	22.5	10.2
48	1:21.0	34.6	22.0	10.0
47	1:19.5	34.0	21.5	9.9
46	1:18.0	33.5	21.1	9.8

To determine quarter-mile time when the endurance time is not on line with speed time, the accompanying chart should be used as a graph. Plot the point of endurance on the scale and the point of speed on the speed scale. More or less bisect the vertical distance between the two with a horizontal line between. Then extend it to intersect the quarter scale, and this will determine the quarter time.

Plotting of times has worked for us in almost every case. Due to a wet and windy spring, Jennings was never able to work his endurance time down to the horizontal line of his sprint speed. He had the following times: 660 - 1:21.6, 330 - 34.4, 220 - 21.9, and 100 - 10.0. If these are plotted on the graph, the result is about 48 or a fraction over. Jennings' best 440 times, mentioned previously, were 48.3 and 48.4.

Hard work cannot be stressed too much, because it is the key to champion quarter-milers. Many boys who run the 100-yard dash in 10.0 or better have never broken 50 seconds in the quarter. Generally, this is the result of poor attitude toward work and self-satisfaction with the short races. For those coaches who like to win and do not have an abundance of prime talent around, the word, *work*, is the key to success. A team that has eight to ten average to good quarter-milers looks good in almost all competition.

8

TRAINING PROGRAM FOR SPRINTERS

Dave Rankin,
Purdue University

The schools of thought pertaining to the make-up of a training program for sprinters seem to change every four or five years. A training program for sprinters, as well as other athletes should be based on technical and common sense information, but not overbalanced in either phase. A degree of technical knowledge is necessary to evaluate the many ideas that common sense tells us might be practical.

Our program for sprinters consists of pre-season, early season, competitive season, and late-competitive season training. The pre-season program starts the development of total body endurance. Early season work tends more toward the development of individual muscle groups, but also has some speed and skill work. The competitive season deals with a mixture of training mentioned, but the concentration is on reaction of movement and progression of skills (technique). The late competitive season is one of concern, and maintaining a type of training.

Pre-Season (4 weeks)

At the start of this season we assume the runners have done no training. The three-day-a-week workout does not seem to be much, but it gives those who are a little too energetic an alternate day to reduce any soreness. The mental and physical development, meanwhile, is gradually progressing.

Monday-Wednesday-Friday

Practice.

Run a mile at easy pace. Do general exercises, and be very cautious on stretching. Run an inclined hill several times. (Steps are a good substitute). Weight training for the upper body. (The weight training is best added after a week or two of practice).

Illustration 1 shows Nate Adams in a good relaxed position at the blocks. He uses a coordinated movement, with his weight properly distributed, to arrive at the get-set position (Illustration 2). The angle of Nate's back leg is correct; his buttocks are higher than his shoulders to provide a better position (Illustration 3). As shown in Illustration 4, his movement is forward with his shoulders rising. Illustration 5 shows good position on the forward block. Good contact with the block in an extended leg drive is shown in Illustration 6. Notice that Adams' torso is rising gradually to a running position. As shown in Illustration 7, use of the blocks has been completed.

Early Season (6 weeks)

The pre-season program will produce enough general body endurance for the early season program.

(First 2 weeks)

Mondays

1 - Warm up, include exercises. 2 - two 220's (estimate 28 second average), jog a 220 between. 3 - Jog, walk, and rest for a combined 6 to 8 minutes. 4 -Repeat No. 2. 5 - Cool down, jogging for 10 minutes.

Tuesdays

1 - Warm up. This is a good time to teach the competition warm-up, keeping all phases of speed running relative to condition. 2 - Weight training. 3 - Jogging.

Wednesdays

1 - Warm up. 2 - Two 660's (runner sets own speed), and then jog, walk, and rest for a combined 15 to 20 minute period in between. 3 - Cool down, jogging for 10 minutes.

Thursdays

1 - Practice competition warm-up. 2 - Weight training. 3 - Jogging.

Fridays

1 - Warm up. 2 - four 60's (accelerations), jogging 160 between. The accelerations are pick-ups without forceful running. 3 - Jog, walk, and rest, for a combined 6 to 8 minutes. 4 - Repeat No. 2. 5 - Repeat No. 3. 6 - Repeat No. 2. 7 - Repeat No. 3. 8 - Jogging.

(Third Week)

Monday

1 - Warm up. 2 - Three 330's (estimate: 220 - :27 to :28, 330 - :42 to :43), jog, walk, and rest for a combined 10 minutes. 3 - cool down jogging.

Tuesday

1 - Warm up, with additional ending buildups. 2 - Instruction on positions in the blocks. 3 - Weight training. 4 - Jogging.

Wednesday

1 - Competition warm-up. 2 - Run 500. The total run is not intended to be an all-out performance. Suggested pace: 220-:28, 330-:43, 440-:57, finishing the last 60 running as hard as form permits. 3 - Cool down, jogging for 10 minutes.

Thursday

1 - Warm-up. 2 - Check positions in blocks. 3 - Weight training. 4 - Jogging.

Fridays

1 - Warm-up. 2 - Four 60's (accelerations, building up stride length), jogging 160 between. The build-ups are not to be full force. 3 - Jog, walk, and rest for a combined 6 minutes. 4 - Repeat No. 2. 5 - Repeat No. 3. 6 - Repeat No. 2. 7 -Jogging.

(Fourth Week)
Monday
1 - Warm up. 2 - two 220's (estimate 26 to 27 sec. average), jog a 220 between. 3 - Jog, walk, and rest for a combined 6 to 8 minutes. 4 - Repeat No. 2. 5 - Cool down, jogging for 10 minutes.
Tuesday
1 - Warm up. 2 - Work out of the blocks, short yardage, without the gun. 3 -Weight training. 4 - Jogging.
Wednesday
1 - Competition warm-up. 2 - Run 330, near full effort. 3 - Jog, walk and rest for a combined 20 to 30 minutes. 4 - Repeat No. 2. 5 - Cool down, jogging for 10 minutes.
Thursday
1 - Warm-up. 2 - Work block positions, but no hard starts. 3 - Weight training. 4 - Jogging.
Friday
1 - Warm-up. 2 - Eight 60's (accelerations without force), jogging 160 between. 3 - Jog, walk, and rest for a combined 10 minutes. 4 - Repeat No. 2. 5 -Jogging.
(Fifth Week)
Monday
1 - Warm-up. 2 - Weight training. 3 - Jogging, running, jogging for 15 minutes.
Tuesday
1 - Warm-up. 2 - Two 330's (reduce the time from the last average), jog, walk, and rest between 15 to 20 minutes. 3 - Cool down, jogging for 10 minutes.
Wednesday
1 - Warm-up. 2 - Weight training. 3 - Jog.
Thursday
1 - Competition warm-up. 2 - Run a 330 trial. Set a 220 pace using Tuesday's 330's as a guide. 3 - Cool down, jogging for 10 minutes.
Friday
1 - Warm-up. 2 - Check block positions, come out slowly several times.
(Sixth Week)
Monday
1 - Warm-up. 2 - Work out of the blocks 10 to 20 yards, no starting signal. 3 - Jogging.
Tuesday
1 - Warm-up. 2 - Work out of the blocks 30 to 40 yards, using starting signal. 3 - Jogging.
Wednesday
1 - Warm-up. 2 - Weight training. 3 - Jogging and easy running.

Thursday

1 - Warm-up. 2 - Work starts if Tuesday's work was not too strenuous. 3 - Jog well.

Friday

1 - Warm-up, exercising, and easy stretching. 2 - Jogging, running and jogging.

Competitive Season

The pre-season and early season programs will have produced general body and muscle endurance. During the competitive season it is necessary to improve endurance progressively. It is also the season in which strength and power become prominent factors.

(First Week)

The first week does not actually include outside competition. It is a good idea to start a week ahead of the competition getting the sprinters mentally and physically adjusted to the rearrangement of the workout days.

Monday

1 - Warm up. 2 - Five 60's (accelerations, without force), jogging 160 between. 3 - Jog, walk, and rest for a combined rest as desired. 4 - Repeat No. 2. 5 - Jogging.

Tuesday

1 - Warm up. 2 - Two 330's (not all-out, reduce average from last two 330's), jog, walk, and rest appropriate time. 3 - Jog.

Wednesday

1 - Competition warm-up. 2 - Practice starts, with gun. 3 - Cool down jogging 10 minutes.

Thursday

1 - Competition warm-up. 2 - Several practice starts, no gun. 3 - Jog.

Friday

1 - Competition warm-up. 2 - Time trials. 3 - Jog.

(Second Week)

Monday

1 - Warm-up. 2 - Five 60's (accelerations, without force), jog 160 between. 3 - Jog, walk, and rest combined 6 to 8 minutes. 4 - Repeat No. 2. 5 - Cool down jogging 10 minutes.

Tuesday

1 - Warm-up. 2 - two 220's (refer to last average), jog 220 between. 3 - Jog, walk, and rest combined 6 to 8 minutes. 4 - Repeat No. 2. 5 - Cool down jogging 10 minutes.

Wednesday

1 - Warm-up. 2 - Check block positions. 3 - General running for rhythm and form.

Thursday
1 - Competition warm up. 2 - Practice starting, with gun. 3 - Baton passing. 4 - Jog.

Friday
1 - Warm up. 2 - Review Saturday's time schedule.

Saturday
Competition

(Remaining Weeks Of Competitive Season)

Mondays
1 - Warm up, an essential part of every session. 2 - Run 60's (accelerations, without force), jogging 160 between. The number of times depends on the progression to date. 3 - Jogging and walking, the amount proportional to the intensity of the workout.

Tuesdays
1 - Warm up. 2 - Run 220's, 330's or 500's according to previously scheduled use. 3 - Jogging and walking.

Wednesdays
1 - Warm up. 2 - Check block positions. 3 - Run 75's (one-half to three-quarters speed) run-throughs, jogging 145 between. The stride should be built up as it is in a race. 4 - Jogging and walking.

Thursdays
1 - Warm up. 2 - Starts with gun, 50 to 60 yards. 3 - Baton passing. 4 - Jogging and walking.

Fridays
1 - Warm up. 2 - Spend additional time warming up if all resistance and tightness is not out of the body. 3 - Check time schedules for Saturday.

Saturday
Competition.

Late Competitive Season

While this season passes very quickly it is as important as any of those previously mentioned.

(Several Weeks)

Monday
1 - Run on the grass. The warm up can be included in the running. The idea is free-lifting runs with no force and no prescribed practice period.

Tuesday
1 - Warm up. 2 - Assigned workout. Make the workout maintaining effort rather than progressive work. Refer to a workout of the competitive season that does not emphasize speed. 3 - Jogging and walking.

Wednesday
1 - Warm up. 2 - Build-ups on the grass. 3 - Jogging.
Thursday
1 - Competition warm up. 2 - Starts with the gun. Work for concentration.
3 - Jog.
Friday
Rest.
Saturday
Competition.

SUMMARY

Pre-season is the beginning of the mental and physical encouragement for the seasons of training and competition. The added encouragement is mental stimulation of the fourth-coming competitive season. It is important in this season to produce a background that will lend to a constant planned progression of training, and during this time a great deal can be accomplished that need not be accented later. The ease with which the season progresses also provides encouragement. Easy running gives an opportunity to reduce body resistance and achieve rhythmic, coordinated, and economical movements. So-called shin splints result from poor running form.

Weight training should be that of upper body development. The upper body will develop more quickly than the lower body, but it gives a feeling of strength that will encourage lower body development. Uphill running conditions and develops the psoas muscle, which is important in the knee lift. This particular development must be accomplished before, not during the competitive season.

In this preliminary stage of conditioning, the program gives the body a chance to rebuild. The circula-respiratory endurance approach not only aids total body endurance, but also prepares for the future intensity of rapid and prolonged action of large muscle groups.

Early season is the time to build all the phases necessary for capacity sprinting. Concentrate on muscle endurance, development of power, and speed of movement. Again, there must be a progression in the development of these phases. Coaches should keep daily workout records, and assign progressive work. During this time the competition warm-up should be thoroughly explained. It should be practiced so that the runner knows the time element involved, and the feeling of intensity that is necessary for capacity performance. A poor warm-up is conducive not only to poor performance, but also to injury.

In any given workout the highest speed of movement during the session should always be done in the next step after the warm-up, regressing then to the second highest speed, etc. There are certain factors which contribute to muscle termperature and muscle fatigue.

A training program for sprinters, as well as for other athletes, should be based on techni-cal and common-sense information, but not overbalanced in either phase.

The competitive season is the objective of all previous work and preparation. Trials are necessary at the competitive distance for a feeling of confidence and security. It is not necessary to run trials during the weeks of competition. Constant work at race pace reduces the nervous reaction, and eventually the body will rebel.

We can acknowledge that speed in inherent. It can be increased by reducing body weight, and perfecting a better execution of technique. When doing any warm-up exercises, it is advisable not to overextend. In some cases, this has a tendency to result in tendon soreness. Furthermore, the cooling down period has valuable assets and should be practiced after each workout session and after each competition.

In the attempt to progress mentally and physically through the seasons, a point is finally reached where the body fails to react to continued work. The runner is, or should be, at this time of the season fully conditioned, and any more work of a progressive nature is useless. Workouts at race intensity are unrewarding as each competition is an effort after the lengthy season. The maintaining effort in a workout should be at a level that is not demanding of the body or spirits.

PART II
THE HURDLES

9

ELIAS GILBERT OVER THE HIGHS

Wilbur L. Ross,
Maryland State College

Illustration 1 shows Gilbert still on the approach side of the hurdle. His weight is beginning to shift forward, and he is starting to raise high on the toe which is still on the ground. His arms are carried waist high so he can get into his body pitch as low as possible. Watch the position of his right arm throughout this series of illustrations. It will act as a guide in helping him maintain his balance.

Gilbert's weight is farther forward (Illustration 2). He is higher on his toes, and his left arm is beginning to move toward its extended position. His lead leg is lifted straight up in front of his body.

The next position (Illustration 3) is assumed just before Elias' body is lifted from the ground. Perfect balance at this point is shown in the lead leg. His head, knee and toe are in perfect alignment. Gilbert is as high on his toe as possible, and his lead leg has moved to its highest position before going into the flight.

Illustration 4 shows Gilbert off the ground and starting to extend his left arm. His head has moved to an advanced position which indicates that the center of gravity has shifted forward. The position of his right arm has changed. His trailing leg is at its first stage in the hip circle.

Early in flight Gilbert's shoulders are squared and he is bending at the waist to the point where his head is directly over the knee of his lead leg (Illustration 5). His lead leg is almost fully extended, and his trailing leg is at a more advanced position in the hip circle. Notice that he appears to be pulling it forward. His right arm is moving downward slightly.

1

2

3

4

5

6

7

8

When he is in full flight (Illustration 6), Gilbert locks his right knee which helps him sail over the hurdle. His trailing leg is moving forward steadily. Elias' right arm is still moving down.

As shown in Illustration 7, Gilbert's body position is almost the same as it was in Illustration 6, with two differences. First, his right arm is moving back on its way to a hooking position that is characteristic of his style. We would not recommend that this form be emulated. Elias' trailing leg has started to rotate, starting into the fourth position split in flight.

At the crest position over the hurdle, Gilbert's lead leg begins to break slightly in a downward position (Illustration 8). His right arm is moving back and his weight is equally distributed at this point of the flight.

Illustration 9 shows that Gilbert has moved to a more advanced position over the barrier. The dropped position of his foot in the lead leg gives rise to his descent. His right hand appears to be placed in an imaginary back pocket. Elias' trailing leg is almost over the top of the barrier, and the position of his trailing toe is everted. His shoulders have remained square, helping him maintain his balance throughout.

9

10

11

12

The point to be noticed in Illustration 10 is the fashion in which the everted toe position helps the trailing knee and ankle pass over the barrier. Gilbert's lead leg appears to be in the first stage of a pawing position. His shoulders are still squared and his body remains flexed at the waist.

As shown in Illustration 11, Gilbert has finally cleared the hurdle, and he is preparing to land in a running position. Notice that his body weight is still well forward, and his balance has not changed.

Elias is starting to straighten up (Illustration 12.). His arms are still close to his body, which tells us he has maintained his balance throughout. His trailing leg has gone to the under-the-arm position, preparing itself for the step-down action.

Balance is present at this point because Gilbert's head, knee, and toe are still in alignment (Illustration 13). This position can be attained only by top performers. Muscle definition in Elias' back is smooth, showing an absence of tension. The pawing action will be terminated as soon as the lead leg strikes the ground.

Gilbert is shown on the ground in Illustration 14. His trailing leg has progressed to the step-down position where it is no longer under his left arm. He is still on his toe. This position is indicative of a ball, toe rolling action which helps him resume the rolling, pushing position while moving forward toward the next barrier.

As he starts off to the next barrier (Illustration 15), Gilbert is the picture of balance, and the pushing action can be seen clearly. Notice the downward driving position of his trailing leg.

13   **14**   **15**

10

HIGH HURDLE ARM ACTION

Tom Ecker,
Cedar Rapids, Iowa, Community Schools

During high hurdle clearance, the action of the trailing leg and the reaction of the leading arm are in parallel planes, around two vertical secondary axes - a lower secondary axis through the hips and an upper secondary axis through the shoulders (Illustration 1).

There is also a vertical primary axis passing through the hurdler's center of mass as he clears the hurdle (Illustration 2), but, ideally, there is no rotation around this primary axis. However, if the hurdler's arm movement is such that there is less reaction in the upper body than there is action from the trailing leg, then the remaining reaction must be absorbed by the body, which can cause the hurdler to twist in the air and land off-balance.

It is true that the high hurdler's forward-leaning trunk increases the rotary inertia around his vertical axis and is able to absorb much of the reaction. However, there is enough twisting caused by the trailing leg during hurdle clearance to require that the arm action provide a reaction that eliminated any twisting of the entire body. Without proper arm action, the hurdler must either land off-balance, or compensate by learning to take off off-balance.

The hurdler's trailing leg contains more mass than either of his arms. Therefore, we must adopt one or a combination of the following techniques in order to provide arm action that is equal and opposite to the action of the trailing leg:

Illustration 1.

Illustration 2.

Illustration 3.

A graphic example of "High hurdle arm action."

• Use both arms in the reaction by having the leading arm forward and the opposite arm back during the take-off (Illustration 3). Then, during hurdle clearance, sweep the leading arm back and the rear arm forward as the trailing leg moves forward.

• Increase the radius of the leading arm during hurdle clearance by keeping the elbow straight and swinging the straightened arm back. This practice is condemned by many coaches, but is practiced, out of necessity, by most hurdlers.

• Increase the arc of the leading arm's backward sweep by having the leading arm in front of the body at take-off, rather than straight ahead. Many top hurdlers are now using this technique.

Any of these techniques will increase rotary inertia (mr^2) around the upper secondary axis and make it possible for the upper body to react equally to the action of the trailing leg.

Speed is not the most important factor in high hurdling.

11

FROM THE FIFTH HURDLE TO THE TAPE

Wilbur L. Ross,
Track Consultant

Athletes, over the years, have been running high hurdles in the most efficient style from the starting blocks to the fifth hurdle and have had very little difficulty in bringing about what would be considered a decent time. But weakened performance after crossing the fifth hurdle and while traversing the second five hurdles of the race has caused a rate of deceleration which in effect cancels out the ability they exhibit in the first portion.

It is our belief that today's athletes can learn to run from the fifth hurdle to the tape with more velocity than they imagine they have to take that distance. The spectator watching the 110-yard high hurdles generally feels that this race is one which requires speed, balance, and rhythm, but we know better. It has been proved consistently that speed is not the most important factor in high hurdling. It is necessary of course, but to be effective it must be accompanied by stamina which will carry the hurdler the full flight and help him maintain the speed he has acquired in the early phases of the race.

Athletes who have exhibited a faulty race in not being able to finish with speed equivalent to that they have carried over the first five hurdles are as follows: Harrison Dillard who was able to run the first five hurdles or 60 yards in 7.1 seconds; Charles Hlad, formerly of Michigan Normal, who was able to run over the first five hurdles in 7.2 seconds but yet was never clocked in 6.2 equivalent time running over the second five; and Hayes Jones, also of Michigan Normal, who was able to run over the first five in 6.8 seconds but never able to put the 5.8 equivalent over the last 60 yards to his race. Along with them could be classified Charles Pratt, formerly of Manhattan College, who ran over the first 60 yard highs in 7.1 seconds but was never able to run better than the 13.8 altogether.

On the other hand, there are those who have been able to put the second 60 yards on an approximate level with what they have done on the first 60 yards together to clock a final time of 13.2 seconds. Elias Gilbert, who had his fastest time of 7.2 seconds, was able to clock as fast as 13.4. Francis Washington, who had a best time of 7.3 seconds, was able to put his second flight of hurdles together to run 13.6. Russell Rodgers, who had a fastest time of 7.3, was able to clock total time of 13.6 seconds.

This latter could be considered a contrasting group because of the fact that none of those mentioned are considered to be men of extra high speed, whereas the first group are men of sprint type ability who were capable of running 9.4 (10.3 seconds) or 9.5 (10.4 seconds) for the 100 yards (100 meters). The second group of men were not capable of doing such but could be clocked in 9.7 (10.6 seconds) on up to 10.9 seconds flat over the same distance mentioned previously.

The momentum necessary to carry through a flight of hurdles in representative time can easily be acquired, and in our opinion we can help these men become proficient in the second part of the 110 hurdles.

● Learn to overemphasize the training day after establishing a form pattern of running the barriers. In books on track and field in the past, authors have advocated that running over three hurdles during a practice session was desirable, but we would like to take issue with this concept. In the indoor hurdle, when the athlete cannot get out on the track, the flight pattern should be as follows: two lanes of five hurdles established somewhere in an indoor arena, field house or gymnasium with the hurdler running back-and-

To be an effective hurdler, an individual should have the stamina to maintain his speed over the complete distance and full flight of hurdles.

forth series, over five hurdles doing the five steps in between each barrier. The general idea on which to concentrate is to build for stamina and form structure by doing series of five steps over the five barriers. This can be increased according to the strength of the hurdler. During the first week of practice, when he is starting to orientate himself in the activity, the athlete should begin programming his work by crossing these barriers 20 times, i.e. 10 flights of round trips up and back over the five sets. As the weeks move along, the round trip requirement is increased and the athlete is asked to go 20, 30, or 40 round trips. Later, as the workouts become more strenuous, the athlete is asked to go 50 or 60 round trips until he has built enough strength, courage and endurance to go 100 round trips. When he has gone 100 round trips, there is no doubt that he has acquired sufficient leg strength and trailing power that running through the second 60 yards on to the tape becomes much easier. The work just outlined is quite strenuous and will cause a great deal of fatigue, but because of this strength work the athlete will gain the necessary power to carry him from the fifth hurdle to the tape with more speed.

● For the second exercise, set up a full flight of hurdles (10) and have the hurdler run this full flight with a time requirement, six times, on alternate days. The time requirement should start at the fastest speed that he possibly could obtain, rhythmically moving down to a speed he desires when fatigue sets in. In other words, let us say the athlete has the ability for 14 seconds flat race. The time requirement of these six sets of 110 hurdles will be as follows: the first set, 14.4 seconds; the fifth one 14.5 seconds; and the last flight, with a longer rest interval, 14.3 seconds. With these sets of six, we know the boy will learn to control his speed and gain the strength necessary to go under 14 seconds very quickly, mainly because he has become physically and psychologically adjusted to the fatigue element that has prevented him from ducking below the 14-second barrier.

● Two running exercises which the athlete must do have been discussed. Now let us go into the light weight training that must take place. The athlete must take the barbells and follow a certain program which is common to us -abdominal sit-ups to develop the muscles of the lower abdomen and lateral leg lifts to strengthen the brevis muscles group located in the area of the groin or, in common terminology, the crotch. When the athlete has given these muscles the proper work, there is no doubt that the fourth position split which he must maintain throughout the exercises previously mentioned will be very easy to execute.

The next exercise the athlete must do is the dumbbell press over the head to strengthen the arms and help him build powerful shoulders. The purpose of building the arm muscles is that it is an important factor in preventing the fatigue element from destroying his perfect balance and timing when he is running over the barriers because his arms are being extended in front of the body constantly and/or moving in a 90° driving fashion while he is running between the hurdles.

Another exercise that might be used is full squats with barbells resting on the shoulders and wooden blocks placed below the heels. Athletes usually are asked to take three sets of ten increasing in number to six sets with short rest intervals.

The last exercise is the trailing leg restrainer, and this is done by having sand bags placed around the legs, at the ankle and the thigh, and the athlete standing beside the barrier doing sets of trailing leg rotations over the side of the hurdle. This will help him build stronger force from the trailing position to the step down, plus helping him fight off fatigue and remedy his inability to run over the last barriers with proficiency.

Another activity that the athlete must learn is the exercise known as the trunk-flexer. The trunk-flexer is one in which he lies on his back and attempts to touch his toes when he brings his body off the floor. He lifts his legs off the floor over his head and simultaneously goes into a half-sitting position extending his arms with the intention of touching his toes.

The whole secret of high hurdling is for the athlete to maintain the form, establish a rhythm pattern which will be equivalent to that of the opponent of better, and run the hurdles from the fifth to the finish line tape stronger than he has run from the blocks to the fifth hurdle, because the race is won at the end of 120 yards (110 meters), and not at 60 yards. Now is the time for him to condition himself to meet the challenge of his rival by being able to accelerate his race from the fifth hurdle to the finish line tape.

12
THE INTERMEDIATES

Del. G. Hessel,
Colorado State University,

The 440 intermediate hurdles is one of the most interesting and difficult events in track and field. An intermediate hurdler must be an athlete of considerable athletic ability and he must have size and strength. The majority of the best intermediate hurdlers such as John Akii-Bua, Dave Hemery, Ralph Mann, Jim Bolding, and others, are over 6 feet tall and weigh more than 160 pounds. They are men who can sprint and high hurdle well and are tenacious competitors. They are mentally tough.

When selecting an intermediate hurdler, a coach might look for a tough half-miler who competes well but cannot get the last 220. His temperament and strength may go well for one lap over the hurdles. The other possibility is to convert a high hurdler who lacks basic speed or technique into an intermediate hurdler.

It is not hard to sell the intermediates to the athlete who has a competitive spirit and a desire for success. The event is obviously a man's race, the challenge is there. It is not an event that is overly crowded with participants. It is an interesting event.

To become a good intermediate hurdler, an athlete must acquire strength, speed, endurance, hurdling technique, hurdling balance, stride patterns, a relaxed running style and an unshakable ability to concentrate. Assuming that the coach's selection is good, the next step is to teach the athlete proper hurdling form. If he is a high hurdler, this is not a difficult task. The intermediate hurdling style is not as aggressive as the high hurdles. It is not slow, but since the hurdle is lower, it is taken off a striding run and one might say it would appear as though he is using the hurdle form in a full 440 stride. The lead leg does not snap down as quickly nor does the trail leg come through too quickly.

If the selected athlete is not a high hurdler, it would be advisable for him to work over the highs for a couple of weeks before going into the intermediates, since the exaggerated high hurdle form will make the intermediates come easier. Most beginning intermediate hurdlers who have not worked the highs have a tendency to take the hurdles too high in a jumping action off the heel. This results in a jarring lead leg action on the far side with the hip dropped and a breaking of momentum. Balance is usually off and the trail leg action lacks the proper layout action. Therefore, by going directly into the intermediates without high hurdle work, the athlete starts out by practicing several improper techniques. However, the high hurdles force him to practice proper hurdle technique.

It should be pointed out that the intermediate hurdler should lead with his left leg. This is important as he takes the hurdles around a turn. A right-leg lead hurdler will drift from the inside of the lane to the outside as he crosses the hurdle on the turn due to centrifugal force. This type of hurdler can lose somewhere between three- to five-tenths in the race.

As the athlete learns intermediate form, it is best to practice first on the straight-away hurdles. Some helpful hints might be:

- Lean into the hurdle but not too aggressively.
- Drop the opposite arm and shoulder down on the lead leg.
- Keep the head forward and straight with the eyes looking down the track.
- The diving action across the hurdle is composed of the forward head lean, body lean, and dropping of the opposite shoulder and forearm down on the lead leg.
- The trail leg is not brought through immediately but rather delayed slightly and lifted. This motion will help the forward lean as the hurdler lands on the other side.
- The trail leg delays and then comes through quickly just before the lead leg contacts the ground. Bringing the trail leg through too quickly can result in a position that is too upright before making contact with the ground.
- Be sure that the hurdler pulls his trail leg completely through with high knee action in order to take a large full stride away from the hurdle.
- Stay up on the toes as much as possible when going into and getting away from the hurdles. Be sure to maintain good forward lean.

Hurdling on the turns is technically the same as it is on the straightaway, except the hurdler's position in relation to the hurdle requires greater concentration and his balance on the hurdle is more difficult. The turns must be practiced over and over before the hurdler will feel comfortable

While working on the hurdles, the coach must constantly remind the hurdler to keep his shoulders squared, hips squared, head carried in a straight line, and his arms in as tight to his body as possible and under control.

Running style in the 440 intermediate hurdles is similar to that of the open 440 except that the intermediate hurdler must continue a smooth attacking of each hurdle in a highly concentrated style.

The next problem to solve is the selection of a stride pattern. It is suggested that the younger athlete use a pattern of 15-17, changing to 17 between the fifth and sixth hurdle. However, there are several stride patterns used such as: 1. Fifteen all the way. 2. Thirteen-15. 3. Fourteen all the way, alternating lead legs. 4. Thirteen-14 alternating near the end.

In counting the number of strides between hurdles such as 13 strides, the hurdler counts a number each time his trail leg contacts the running surface. The decision as to when to change from 13 to 15 or 15 to 17 depends upon the endurance of the athlete. If a younger hurdler is caught between a certain stride pattern, the coach should encourage him to work towards the pattern of fewest strides rather than shorten up. With work and experience, the hurdler will soon adjust to the pattern. It should be mentioned that overstriding can result in a loss of time just as understriding can. For obvious reasons it appears as though the best stride pattern would be 13 all the way. The second best pattern would probably be a 13-14 pattern, alternating lead legs as the last two or three hurdles are taken.

Most good intermediate hurdlers change from 13 to 15 between the sixth and seventh hurdles. However, this is not necessarily the best for all hurdlers since some can carry the 13-step stride pattern longer. A hurdler should not give up on the pattern of fewest strides until fatigue forces him to change. When the change does take place, it must be done with concentration and completed quickly and smoothly after clearing the last hurdle. Being fatigued and running up on a hurdle (chopping) will cause a breaking of valuable momentum and probably cost the hurdler the race.

The stride pattern to the first hurdle is different from the other hurdles. When preparing for the start, the lead leg is back in the blocks. It usually takes 21 to 22 steps to the first hurdle but this depends on the hurdler's stride length, and the number could go as high as 24. A right-leg lead can present problems in the hurdling position, since the hurdler would like to run the curve as tightly as possible. But if this position is held over the hurdle, the left trail leg will drag around the hurdle resulting in disqualification. The left lead leg hurdler does not have this problem.

Running style in the 440 intermediate hurdles is similar to that of the open 440 except that the intermediate hurdler must continue a smooth attacking of each hurdle in a highly concentrated style. Any deceleration is difficult to recover, especially near the end of the race.

There is only one way to run the 440 intermediate hurdle race and that is as fast and as effortless as possible. It is imperative that the hurdler attack the first two hurdles. This method will get his momentum going and allow him to settle into his rhythm or stride as quickly as possible. A good intermediate hurdler should be able to run his intermediate race within two seconds, or close to two seconds, of his best open quarter. The first 220 should come quickly, fly by. The next 220 requires great concentration. As fatigue sets in, the athlete must relax and concentrate on holding good form (arms pumping, knees up, striding well, correct lean, and good balance on the hurdle). Hurdles eight, nine and ten can look 10 feet tall as the legs tire. Those barriers have eliminated more potential winners than any others. This is most generally due to the opponent, a lack of concentration or a registration of tiring. If the hurdler does manage the last hurdles well, he can still make an error by becoming overanxious to sprint off the last hurdle. This failure to clear the last hurdle smoothly can result in a loss of balance, momentum and the race.

Training used for the intermediates should be a combination of strength and speed. The hurdler must have the speed of a good quarter-miler and the strength of a good half-miler. Workouts should be a combination of intervals, hurdling, and overdistance. One important factor to remember is that effective hurdling requires good strength, and the workout previous to a hurdle day should be reasonably light.

There are a great variety of possible workouts: 5 x 2 hurdles; 5 x 5 hurdles; 4 x 440 hurdles with only hurdles 8, 9, 10 up; and 1 x 5 hurdles. All hurdling requires full effort.

Interval training can be similar to that of a half-miler. In fact, the hurdler may work with middle distance men when he is not hurdling.

The entire training season should progress from quantity to quality. The hurdler should be involved in cross-country type training during the fall along with some interval and hurdling work. During the indoor season the intermediate hurdler should compete in the half-mile, 600 or quarter-mile.

Important Facts

- The steps to the first hurdle can range from 21 to 24.
- The steps between hurdles can range from 13 to 17.
- It is 147 feet, 9 inches to the first hurdle.
- It is 139 feet, 6 inches to the finish from the tenth hurdle.
- It is 114 feet, 9 inches between the hurdles.
- An intermediate hurdler should be able to run his race somewhere between 2 and 5 seconds of his best open quarter.
- It takes a good intermediate hurdler about 6.0 to get over the first hurdle. This time can range from 5.8 to 6.5.
- Getting in between the hurdles can range from 4.1 to 4.6.
- The split between the first and second 220 should range from one to two seconds.
- It takes about 5 seconds to finish the race from the tenth hurdle.
- The intermediate hurdle is 36 inches high.

13

GETTING THE MOST FROM THE INTERMEDIATES

Dixon Farmer,
Occidental College

One of the most neglected and misunderstood track and field events is the 440 intermediate hurdles. At both the high school and college levels the lack of coaching and participation becomes increasingly evident each year. In 1968 the world, American, European, Olympic, collegiate, junior collegiate, and high school records were obliterated. The wholesale annihilation might lead one to say that the records previous to 1968 were not of high quality and, with the added impetus of the Olympic games, they were plums to be picked off by any number of superb athletes. We believe that if the type of concentration on the intermediate hurdles which previously existed only in Olympic years became the norm, then the global and national records in the hurdles would finally reach the level that other events now enjoy.

Only through increased knowledge and subsequent appreciation of the intermediates can this former orphan become an event to challenge the glamour of the other popular track and field events.

The first step in the training of an intermediate hurdler is the recognition of his qualifications for the event. Hurdlers come in a multitude of sizes and shapes and represent almost the entire scale of abilities ranging from the speed of sprinters to the endurance of milers and from a triple jumper's resiliency to a shot putter's strength. To point at any one athlete and decide that he will be an intermediate hurdler is a mistake.

As an example, the top ten American intermediate hurdlers at Lake Tahoe in 1968 had as composite abilities, a 9.5 (100), 20.8 (220), 1:48.6 (880), 14:0 (120 high hurdles), 47'11" (triple jump), and a 14'0" (pole vault). Some hurdlers had little speed but good staying power, others the opposite. Some were fine high hurdlers, others could not negotiate a 42" barrier. This versatility, as valuable as it may have seemed, might also have been a liability. The athletes who won the medals in Mexico City were specialists. Hemery, Sherwood, and Hennige probably had the same ability as the previously mentioned Americans, but they spent most of their time specializing in the intermediate hurdles. Our system of collegiate dual meet competition does not allow this specialization. Very few American medium hurdlers do not have to run a 440, the highs, an 880, a relay or two and then the intermediates, thus spreading their talent rather thin.

This is not a suggestion for a change, only an attempt to answer the question regarding the apparent *slippage* of the United States hurdlers in Mexico City.

With the realization that an intermediate hurdler is difficult to spot at first, some thought must be given to training.

The year is best divided into four segments: summer (June - September); fall (September - November); winter (November - February); and spring (February - June).

The summer training period is a time in which to have some fun, participate in all-comers meets, experiment with other events, but stay active and maintain muscle tone.

The fall period is one in which the work becomes more serious. Beginning on a three- to four-day per week program, the hurdler starts to work on building the all-important endurance which will help him through many intermediate hurdles races. The fall program should consist of a blending of 4-to 6-mile road runs, repeat hill running, weight training, and low intensity interval running such as 10 to 10 x 110 or 150 yards on a grassy, flat area or 8 to 10 x 250 to 300 yards. Using no watch and no pressure, we slowly construct a base on which the competitive season is built.

As winter approaches, the outdoor season is around the corner, and it is at this time that the intensity of the hurdler's training increases. Now the work week is increased to 5 to 6 days. Work is much more pointed and is aimed directly at the intermediate hurdles. Whereas before he might have been a training companion for the 440 or 880 man, now the hurdler embarks on a program of his own.

Bearing in mind that the winter months take us right up to the competitive season, it is in this period that the athlete begins to hurdle at least twice a week and runs interval flat training twice per week. Alternate days find him on the roads, in the parks or easing through the nearby hills. An example of a week in January would be as follows:

Monday - Hard interval training with an emphasis on overdistance: Breakdown - 600 or 4 x 660 between 1:34 and 1:37, 550, 440, 330, and 220.

Tuesday - Hard hurdle training with an emphasis on short, snappy drills: Run 10 x hurdles 1 and 3 from the blocks or 5 x hurdles 1 and 4 and 5 x hurdles 7 and 10.

Wednesday - Generally, this is a relaxing day away from the track. The hurdlers run 4 to 5 miles on a grassy surface or take an easy shuffle through the hills.

Thursday - Hurdle training with an emphasis on longer drills: Run 4 x hurdles 1 and 4, keep moving without the hurdles down the backstretch and then over hurdles 8 and 10 and on to the finish. The total distance is 440 yards or 4 x 220 without hurdles at 27 to 28 pace and then into hurdles 6 and 10, and on to the finish for a total distance of 440 yards. Or the drill can consist of 4 x hurdles 1 and 2, skip 3 and 4, hurdle 5 and 6, skip 7 and 8, hurdle 9 and 10, and on to the finish for a total distance of 440 yards.

This day is important in that it gives the hurdler a chance to hurdle while he is fatigued, and to cover the entire distance of his race. Occasionally they go as far as eight hurdles, but rarely farther and never farther once the season is underway. The psychological strain is too great to complete a workout at race pace, which is necessary when staying with the 13 or 15 stride pattern.

Friday is another change of pace day in that the workout is more relaxed and is often left to the discretion of the athlete. One athlete may feel he needs more hurdling, while another wants to end the week with some interval training, and still another may desire a Fartlek through the country.

Hurdlers come in a multitude of sizes and shapes and represent almost the entire scale of abilities ranging from the speed of sprinters to the endurance of milers and from a triple jumper's resiliency to a shot putter's strength.

With the approach of the competitive season, which ranges from late February until mid-June, we are reaching the top of the pyramid, so to speak. The base has been laid, strength has been gained, the bulk of the endurance work is behind the hurdlers, and now technique and an application of speed work dominate our thoughts.

Generally, the competitive effort comes on Friday and Saturday each week. As a result, the workouts build from Monday to Wednesday and then begin to taper off on Thursday.

Some examples of workouts during the peak weeks of track meets:

Monday - this is an intense speed day, generally done without hurdles. The hurdlers run 3 x 330 with almost a full rest interval at close to top speed, or a 110 - 220 - 330 - 440 build up. This work is done at a rapid pace with a long recovery period.

Tuesday - This is the hardest hurdling day of the week. The work consists of 5 x 220 over hurdles at race pace, or 5 hurdles and rest, then 4 hurdles rest, 3 hurdles rest, and then 2 hurdles. One repetition.

Wednesday - Hurdling and flat training are combined with the hurdling almost always coming last in order to have the athlete hurdle when he is tired. The hurdlers run 2 x 220 flat at rapid speed and then 2 x 5 hurdles; or 6 x 110 flat at rapid speed and then 4 x 3 hurdles.

Thursday - The intensity is lessened quite noticeably and may vary from 4 to 5 miles easy (7:00 min. per mile pace) cross-country run and finish over some hurdles to what we call *round trippers.* The latter entails setting up 6 or 8 hurdles 10 to 15 yards apart on the football field, so there is a hurdle facing each direction. Then the athlete moves over these in a *round trip* or back and forth until he has covered 8 to 10 trips. This is a good warm-up drill as well as a conditioner. Rest 10 minutes and repeat.

Friday - This is either a competitive day or the day before a competition. A long strenuous warm-up including some hurdling and some straight-away running in spikes is scheduled.

Having discussed the recognition of an intermediate hurdler and his subsequent training program, now the form used in clearing the intermediate hurdles will be described. As the name of the event implies, hurdle clearance is a middle road between the dive style of the highs and the erect trunk carriage seen in the low hurdle race. The key to hurdle clearance in the intermediates is continuance of momentum. Although it would not be wise to make a general all-encompassing statement about intermediate hurdle clearance, because it seems almost individual in nature, it is worthwhile to stress momentum continuation. By this is meant that each stride must be a well-balanced, offensive running stride. A major problem arises, for instance, when the hurdler feels the need to gather or settle his hips a bit two or three strides before the intermediate hurdle. He has slowed himself down and discontinued his momentum. It is almost common to see a hurdler coming off the hurdle in poor balance, especially around the turn. His arms have counteracted centrifugal force, pulling the athlete to the outside around the bend. As a result, his trunk headed to the right while his legs were going left. These mistakes call for more defensive striding and getting back into the proper cadence.

We favor the combination. Although there are pros and cons regarding both stride patterns, here are few favoring the 13-stride approach:

1. At the start the athlete is a bundle of nervous energy. Why ask him to do anything but explode that energy at the beginning of his race? A coach with some experience knows that an athlete who runs 25 seconds for his first 220 in a 440 is just as fatigued as the athlete who has run 24, yet he is 6 to 8 yards behind the one who selected the faster pace.

2. In answer to those who say there is too much energy used trying to negotiate the first few hurdles in 13 strides, the point is there is more energy used up by chopping stride at the first 3 or 4 hurdles, draining energy from the quadriceps muscle group by putting on the brakes. These athletes who are strong enough and have developed the proper rhythm and the 7'10" stride necessary for 13 strides, are doing themselves a disservice in not making the attempt.

3. Competitively speaking, the most valid reason to go to 13, if possible, in the early portion of the race, is that it applies pressure on the other hurdles in the race. How often do we see a hurdler lose his concentration and rhythm as another athlete moves up on his inside after having made up the better part of the original stagger. This is a valuable offensive strategy, it should be added to his psychological arsenal.

Running a quarter of a mile over ten 36" barriers at close to top speed is one of the most grueling physical and psychological tests an athlete can face. The more a hurdler understands what he is doing and the better his preparation is, the greater are his chances for passing that test.

14

STRETCHING EXERCISES FOR THE HIGH HURDLES

Tom Ecker,
Cedar Rapids, Iowa, Community Schools

Because of the complexity of his event, the high hurdler must work much harder than the ordinary short-distance runner. He must work not only on improving his physical condition, but must also spend many additional hours perfecting his technique, a phase of running that is more important in hurdling than in any of the other track events.

Hurdling places an unnatural strain on certain skeletal muscles. Therefore each of these muscles must be loosened gradually before every workout session or race. Some of the better muscle-stretching exercises are as follows:

★ Kick high with each leg; gradually at first - then more vigorously (Illustration 1).

★ Sit on the ground in the hurdling position and bend forward (Illustration 2).

★ From a standing position, pull the trail knee up to the chest (Illustration 3).

★ Standing with the lower half of the trail leg resting along the top bar of the hurdle, bend forward and touch the ground with the left hand (Illustration 4).

★ Facing a high hurdle, place the lead foot on the top bar of the hurdle and bend forward, touching the lead foot with the lead hand (Illustration 5).

★ While standing with both hands on the top bar of a high hurdle, swing the trail leg on up through the trailing position and back to the ground several times in succession.

Illustration #1.

Illustration #2.

Illustration #3.

Illustration #4.

Illustration #5.

Illustration #6.

A good culminating exercise is the five-step warm-up between hurdles. The athlete jogs between the highs, taking five steps between them, and emphasizes his forward lean as he drives over each hurdle.

While doing his stretching exercises, the hurdler must remember that none of these should ever be done in a sudden or violent manner. The athlete must develop his looseness gradually, never pushing an exercise past the point of slight strain.

15

THIRTY RUSSIAN FLEXIBILITY EXERCISES FOR HURDLERS

Bob Ehrhart,
Drake University

Athletes from the Soviet Union are among the most limber in the world because they spend so much practice time working on flexibility exercises. Hurdlers, especially, have long routines of stretching exercises that precede each day's practice. Often, early in the season, entire practice sessions are devoted entirely to flexibility exercises.

Beginners must be careful to begin easily, applying only small amounts of stretch to the muscles and joints at first. Then, as the body gains flexibility, additional stretch can be added.

1. While bracing his hands against a wall, with his arms parallel to the ground, the hurdler alternates swinging his knees forward and up.

2. While balanced on his shoulders, or while on his back, the hurdler alternates swinging his knees toward his head.

3. He bends backwards, arching his back, and grabbing his ankles.

4. While bracing the hand against the wall, stand on one leg and swing the free leg back and forward, with the knee bent.

5. With the feet braced against stall bars, alternate bending forward over a side horse and stretching upward with the back arched.

6. Sit on the edge of a table and alternate swinging the legs upward, with the knees straight.

7. While bracing the hand against a wall, swing the free leg backwards, grabbing the ankle of the free hand and pulling the leg upward.

8. While bracing the hand against a wall, continue swinging the free leg through the entire motion of a running stride.

9. While lying on the back, with the knees straight, alternate swinging each leg across the body, touching the opposite hand with the toes.

10. While a teammate holds his ankles, the hurdler alternates arching his back over a horse and raises into a sitting position.

11. Brace one leg against the stall bars and bend to the side, attempting to achieve angles of 90 degrees.

12. While bracing the hand against a wall, swing the free leg in a circle, attempting to keep the knee straight.

13. While bracing the hand against a wall, swing the free leg up, as high as possible, with the knee straight.

14. While holding onto the top bar of a hurdle, lift the free leg above the hurdle and alternate bending and straightening the leg.

15. Hold the top bar of a hurdle and swing the free leg forward and back, with the knee bent.

16. Place the lead leg on the top bar of a hurdle and pull the body forward, bending the knee.

17. Stand beside a hurdle, placing the free foot on top, and bend forward.

18. Stand beside a hurdle, placing the lower leg on top, and bend forward.

19. Do the sprinter's stretch, with arms folded. Bend the upper body downward, touching the head to the ground.

20. Hold onto the stall bars and swing the free leg backward and forward, with the knees bent.

21. The hurdler braces his free leg on the stall bars, as high as he can reach, straightens his leg, and bends forward.

22. With the free leg on the top bar of a hurdle, alternate bending forward and backward.

23. Do the hurdlers' stretch, with the trailing foot next to the hip and the knee elevated. Bring the head and the knee to the ground, keeping the back arched.

24. Do the hurdler's stretch, with the thighs, trailing thigh and trailing calf, and trailing foot, all at 90 degree angles. Bend backwards to the ground, with the arms extended sideways.

25. Lock arms with a teammate , while sitting on the ground, and alternate bending forward.

26. Stand on a set of still rings, holding onto the cables, and alternate stretching the legs forward and back.

27. While the hurdler is lying on his stomach and arching his back, a teammate helps the hurdler grab his ankles.

28. While lying on his back, the hurdler alternates raising his legs into a vertical position, bracing his hips with his hands, and lowering his feet to the ground while his back is arched.

29. Practice the hurdling motion with the trail leg while holding onto stall bars.

30. While holding onto stall bars, practice the hurdling recovery step by pulling the trail leg fron a resting position on a hurdle and driving the knee upward.

PART III

THE

MIDDLE

DISTANCES

16

MIDDLE DISTANCE RUNNING

Bill Huyck,
Carleton College

No coach can watch Mike Boit run by, strong, fluid, and swift, without having a nagging question or two enter his mind. Is it just that he is a rare, superior man or are his superb performances the result of training? What does the training of this great athlete have to offer our team?

Performance of the quality of Mike Boit's can come only from a combination of rare physical and psychological attributes and from proper training.

In considering the training of Boit, or any other great athlete, what can a coach apply to his athletes in his particular situation? Or, for that matter, from among the reams of research and more subjective writing on middle distance training, what can we use now? To whom do we listen - exercise physiologists, LSD advocates, marathon training fanatics or interval freaks? Are there some basic principles or ideas that coaches can adapt to their coaching situations?

First, it is necessary to agree on proper goals for middle distance training in developing the athlete. We suggest that among these might be making satisfying progress towards ultimate performance, encouraging the runner to enjoy his sport and to stay with it long enough to approach ultimate performance.

Winning or running a specific time in a certain season may not be the right goal. For some it is practically impossible, for many others it may not be demanding enough, and it may be just too short-term in nature for a primary goal. Perhaps these things should be considered within or as part of the first two goals mentioned.

We have little enthusiasm for the high school coach who, surrounded by trophies, expresses little interest in or concern for the running his athletes may do in the future. Frankly, we have always wondered what this type of individual would do if the junior high schools in his school system were staffed by coaches of the same philosophy. Some coaches believe in exploiting youthful enthusiasm to the utmost for the time being and forget the future. Those who look to age group swimming, with world records turned in by adolescents who retire at 16, as a model for track and field have a very narrow vision.

Given some agreement on goals, then we suggest there are a few important ideas that can be put to use in any training program:

● There is no short cut to conditioning. Any so-called crash program has built into it sufficient potential for physical injury or discouragement to make its use questionable for most athletes. Good conditioning is generally the result of a prolonged period of gradually progressing moderate efforts.

● The coach should promote off-season running. This is vital to a successful middle distance program. Also, he should encourage other good athletic activities such as swimming, tennis, cross-country, skiing, handball, etc. They will contribute to the physical development of the athlete and provide a refreshing change of pace.

● In training, as well as in competition, it is worthwhile to remember that most athletes, for whatever reason, have no idea how good they can be or how much they can do. Some are simply ignorant of their physical capability, some use modest targets as a defense against failure, and others have been tested when they were not ready and are conditioned to mediocrity. Each day must be an exercise not only in running, but in opening up the athletes' minds to their potential for great achievements. They must be consciously and continually encouraged to see their limits as open-ended....a little better this week than last, appreciably better this year than last, and infinitely better in the long run.

● Regardless of the event, from the 880 to three miles, it might be well to concentrate first on building up aerobic capacity. Long, easy runs, longer easy runs, and eventually, much longer easy runs are a sound basis from which to start.

● Within the general idea of concentrating first on aerobic training and later in the season moving to anaerobic emphasis as the athlete's primary events suggest, the coach should try to utilize a variety of methods. We suggest, long easy continuous runs, faster continuous runs of less duration, slow, easy intervals, Fartlek, faster intervals, sprint training, some time trials at various distances, pace development work, etc. Every means possible should be used to accomplish the purpose.

● Vary not only the training method, but the location and pattern as well. If at all possible, keep the runners off the track. Train on roads and on the

There is no short cut to conditioning.

grass. Run up and down short hills and long ones. Use the beaches, parks, trails, and fields. Do everything to avoid falling into a pattern.

● Have faith in hard work which is well planned and do a great deal of it. The total amount and quality of running done can not only give considerable physiological benefits, but it must also be a source of confidence and pride.

● However, every training session is not a test of an athlete's character or masculinity. There is a large place in the training program for work within but close to his present capabilities. The slowest pace to stimulate maximum oxygen uptake - perhaps 70 per cent or slightly less - seems to have considerable aerobic benefits. Why not increase the total work done by running easily and comfortably at this pace, especially early in the season and on light days?

● There is also a place for extremely demanding, high-intensity training, but it should not be very frequent and the days for it should be chosen carefully. These maximum days help the athlete test himself, build his tolerance for pain and self-punishment, and leave him wiser, proud, and confident. Select these days carefully and use them well.

● A majority of interval training, especially in early and mid-season, might include work segments of at least 2 to 3 minutes duration for optimal aerobic gain. Other intervals might include work segments of 90 seconds or less, or such intensity that during a 90-second recovery jog the heart rate drops to 120 or 130.

● Run in groups. Plan the training to encourage this whenever possible. In doing so, runners share the laughs, rain, pain, satisfaction, and constantly stimulate each other to do better than they would individually. Give support to younger or inexperienced runners by placing them with more experienced men or in a more structured training situation with the coach.

● Be alert for the individual whose needs vary from those of the group, and consistent with the interests of the team, try to help him. Some runners need periodic time trials, some need two light days after a hard day, and some run best when competing only every second week, etc. Identify these athletes as soon as possible, help them if it is possible, and the entire team will benefit.

● Encourage keeping a training diary or log. It will help the coach evaluate training and progress, and, more important, encourage the athlete to think about his training, note his progress, and take more responsibility.

● Training cannot be discussed without considering competition. We feel many athletes suffer as a result of running meets before they are ready and from participating in too many meets. In the long run, it may be preferable to leave a runner out of some early season meets and have him train until he is ready to perform at a decent level and get some satisfaction out of the meet. Similarly, what is the purpose of two meets a week? Does a runner really gain in competitive experience and discipline or is this practice simply an unfortunate carry-over from those who think everything should be modeled after basketball? Are the round-robin duals and triangulars common in many leagues productive or would not less frequent meets encourage better competitive learning, more time for training, and ultimately better performance?

● A pre-meet briefing is not the place to sell the coach's philosophies; every training day is. If he emphasizes, say, an even pace, then he should consciously encourage runners to begin a given workout in a disciplined manner and really drive the middle of the workout. If he wants a cross-country team to run in groups, then sell them on the training field. Designate who will be running with whom at various stages of the workout and when one can take off and break up the group if that is desired. Finishing a long run with a good kick or really driving the last interval or two can often be a good habit regardless of a runner's race tactics.

● Appreciate the value of active rest, particularly in the late season. More important, late season races have been lost because of overwork in the last week or two than because of too much rest. If a runner is not in shape by late season, chances are he is not going to be.

● A thorough, gradual cool-down of walking and jogging after training each day will really pay off in avoiding or reducing stiffness and soreness the next day.

The training of a distance runner may seem relatively simple and objective to the outsider. On the contrary, it includes a fantastic number of physiological and psychological variables, some of which were mentioned in this article.

17

AN APPROACH TO YEAR ROUND TRACK CONDITIONING

Douglas E. Hansen,
Hillsdale College

Several years ago while stationed in Venezuela as a Peace Corps volunteer working for the Venezuelan national government, we had as part of our duties the upgrading of their track and field program. To accomplish the task, we prepared a training philosophy. At the present time, the same basic program is being used in teaching a course in Theory of Track and Field and in explaining to our track athletes the need for year around training.

The program is based on three concepts:
- To become a distance runner, the athlete must run all year.
- One year is only a part of a training program. It must be engaged in for four years and then on into later life.
- Each year's training must have a goal.

The training program attempts to incorporate these concepts and is broken down into four basic periods of time as follows:
- Physical conditioning period (about 5 months).
- Technical conditioning period (4 to 6 weeks).
- The competitive period (about 5 months).
- Active rest period (4 to 6 weeks).

These four periods have specific purposes. The physical conditioning period is a base building period for the athlete and emphasis is placed on quantity as compared to quality. The runner is building a base through running miles and engaging in training to strengthen his muscles, tendons, ligaments, and the entire cariovascular system so he will be ready for the competitive period. Two-a-day workouts are considered normal during the period.

The technical conditioning period is really a transition period from the heavy quantity mileage to the quality interval training. During this period, emphasis is placed on initiating competition to encourage extensive work on techniques, and begin speed work. There is also a decline in total mileage as quality workouts are established.

The competitive period is a quality period. Emphasis is placed on maintaining the base, and building to a top performance. Mileage is also reduced and more interval training is done with the number of overdistance days being determined by the coach. Generally speaking, there is only one workout per day, but this will vary from runner to runner according to the accompanying chart.

The active rest period is the time when the runner makes another transition. The athlete does not engage in competition and is encouraged to have fun. There is nothing specifically scheduled during this time. The runner does what he feels he needs to do before resuming the hard work of the physical conditioning period.

Throughout this discussion no specifics have been given as to types of training and mileage. There are several reasons, but most important is the

The competitive period is the quality period.

fact that each coach has his own basic program which he can modify to the annual program. General activities are listed on the chart. As an example, quantity workouts are specified by long, slow distance, cross-country of Fartlek (speed play). Specific recommendations for weekly workouts must be determined by the coach and the athlete. The chart can help a coach explain the period and the type of training in which the athlete is engaged.

While techniques are shown on the chart for the technical conditioning and competition periods, this does not mean they are not emphasized by the coach at other times. However, it is easier for the athlete to concentrate on techniques such as the knee lift, hill climbing, passing, arm carriage, breathing, etc., once he is in shape.

The purpose of the program is to build a young man totally. It provides him with the strength he needs to grow as a distance runner over the years. In addition, it provides for steady development. Runners are not developed over-night. They need a program which is consistent, rational, and easy to understand. If a runner sees the program laid out he will have greater faith in it and in what he has to do to accomplish his goals.

Chart I
Training Program For Track And Field

About 5 Months	4 or 6 Weeks	About 5 Months	3 or 4 Weeks
7-14 Times a Week	7-10 Times a Week	7 Times a Week	6 Times a week
Physical Conditioning Period	Technical Conditioning Period	Competition Period	Active Rest Period
Hard Physical Training (Circuit Training)	Techniques	Keeping Conditioning	Easy Running
Weight Lifting	Speed Work	Competing in Progressive Intensity	Cross-Country
Endurance Work (Long Slow Distance)	Timing Work (Intervals)	Techniques (Knee Lift)	Free Training
Long Fartlek	Short Fartlek	Speed Work	Games
Long Cross-Country	Short Cross-Country	Timing Work (Fast Intervals)	Recreation
	Begin Competition	Fartlek Cross Country— 1 Time Per Week	

18

PROGRESSIVE INTERVAL TRAINING

Tom Ecker,
Cedar Rapids, Iowa, Community Schools

For many years it has been known that interval training - the program of repeat running that includes a set interval of recovery after each run - is the most effective single training system ever devised. Yet, unfortunately, most interval training programs have become complicated guessing games for the coaches.

There are four factors in any interval training program - the *distance* of the individual runs, the *speed* with which the distance is to be covered, the *length of the recovery* between runs, and the *number* of repetitions.

Most coaches list all four factors as absolutes when putting together each day's training program. For example, a workout for milers might be listed as 20 x 220 @ :35 w/220 jog. But, how do coaches know that 20 is the best number, that 220 is the proper distance, that :35 is the correct speed, and that a 220 jog affords sufficient recovery? More often than not, they do not know.

However, by adopting a program of *progressive* interval training, all of the guessing can be eliminated. With simple substitutions, the coach can use the progressive interval training formula to devise a number of training schedules, without having to worry about making a wrong decision on any of the four interval training factors.

Factor No. 1 - Distance

The distance selected for any progressive interval training session remains constant throughout the workout, but may vary greatly from one workout to the next. The important thing is that the distance is shorter than the athlete's race distance, usually in multiples of 110 yards (or 100 meters).

The distance of each run must be long enough to increase the runner's heart rate for at least 15 seconds, but not so long that the increased heart rate is maintained for more than two minutes. Chart I includes the most common workout distances used when training for the 880, the mile or the two mile.

Chart 1. Workout Distances		
880	Mile	2-Mile
110	110	
220	220	220
330	330	330
440	440	440
660	660	660

Factor No. 2 - Speed

The speed of each repeat run is determined by the runner's projected race pace. The coach predicts the time for the athlete's next competitive race, being careful to take the athlete's ability and present physical condition into consideration. The speed of the repeat runs (the projected racing pace) is determined from that prediction. For example, a 5:00 miler would run repeat 330's in 56 seconds (Chart 2).

Running at pace increases the heart rate to the most beneficial training level (approximately 15 to 20 strokes below maximum), and has the added advantage of helping the runner develop a sense of pace consciousness.

Factor No. 3 - Length of Recovery

For interval training to be a truly effective system for conditioning the runner's circulo-respiratory system, the heart rate must be alternately increased during the runs, and decreased to a level of semi-recovery between runs.

Rather than have the athlete walk or jog for a predetermined period of time during the recovery phase (or for the time it takes to jog for a predeter-

Chart 2 - Pace Chart

Projected Race Time			Workout Speed				
880	Mile	2-Mile	110's	220's	330's	440's	660's
1:44			:13	:26	:39	:52	1:18
1:46					:39.5	:53	1:19.5
1:48			:13.5	:27	:40.5	:54	1:21
1:50					:41	:55	1:22.5
1:52			:14	:28	:42	:56	1:24
1.54					:42.5	:57	1:25.5
1:56	3:52		:14.5	:58	1.27		
1:58	3:56				:44	:59	1:28.5
2:00	4:00		:15	:30	:45	1:00	1:30
2:02	4:04				:45.5	1:01	1:31.5
2:04	4:08		:15.5	:31	:46.5	1:02	1:33
2:06	4:12	8:24			:47	1:03	1:34.5
2:08	4:16	8:32	:16	:32	:48	1:04	1:36
2:10	4:20	8:40			:48.5	1:05	1:37.5
2:12	4:24	8:48	:16.5	:33	*9.5	1:06	1:39
2:14	4:28	8:56			:50	1:07	1:40.5
2:16	4:32	9:04	:17	:34	:51	1:08	1:42
2:18	4:36	9:12			:51.5	1:09	1:43.5
2:20	4:40	9:20	:17.5	:35	:52.5	1:10	1:45
2:22	4:44	9:28			:53	1:11	1:46.5
2:24	4:48	9:36	:18	:36	:54	1:12	1:48
2:26	4:52	9:44			:54.5	1:13	1:49.5
2:28	4:56	9:52	:18.5	:37	:55.5	1:14	1:51
2:30	5:00	10:00			:56	1:15	1:52.5
2:32	5.04	10:08	:19	:38	:57	1:16	1:54
2:34	5:08	10:16			:57.5	1:17	1:55.5
2:36	5:12	10:24	:19.5	:39	:58.5	1.18	1.57
2:38	5:16	10:32			:59	1:19	1:58.5
2:40	5:20	10:40	:20	:40	1:00	1:20	2:00
2:42	5:24	10:48			1:00.5	1:21	
2:44	5:28	10:56	:20.5	:41	1:01.5	1:22	
2:46	5:32	11:04			1:02	1:23	
2:48	5:36	11:12	:21	:42	1:03	1:24	
2:50	5:40	11:20			1:03.5	1:25	
	5:44	11:28	:21.5	:43	1:04.5	1:26	
	5:48	11:36			1:05	1:27	
	5:52	11:44	:22	:44	1:06	1:28	
	5:56	11:52			1:06.5	1:29	
	6:00	12:00	:22.5	:45	1:07.5	1:30	

mined period of time during the recovery distance), it is best to have the athlete repeat the run as soon as the heart rate has decreased to an accurately measured recovery level - usually 120 beats per minute. By measuring the athlete's heart rate after each run, the coach does not have to worry about beginning the following run before the heart rate has decreased enough (or after it has decreased too much) for the workout to be effective.

Heart rate per minute can be computed in a number of ways. Probably the most common is the six-second method. The coach counts the runner's pulse rate for six seconds, and adds a zero. For example, 12 heartbeats in six seconds equals 120 heartbeats per minute, 17 heartbeats in six seconds equals 170 etc. The best way to count heartbeats is by placing the thumb and fingers lightly on either side of the windpipe, the carotid artery, just below the jaw, and count the pulsations.

A more accurate method of computing heart rate per minute is to time 10 heartbeats and use the conversion table shown in Chart 3. The coach starts the watch on a zero count and stops it on the tenth beat following. Or, the coach can place the watch on a table near the starting line and let the athletes check themselves.

A quicker way of determining whether the heart rate has decreased to 120 is to use the 10-heartbeat/5-second method. If on the athlete's tenth heartbeat the stop watch sweep hand stops before the five-second mark, the runner should continue walking or jogging. If the hand stops after the five-second mark, it is time to repeat the run.

Factor No. 4 - Number

Deciding the number of runs to be taken in any particular interval training workout has always been the biggest guessing game the coach has had to play. More often than not, the pre-selected number is either too low, reducing the effectiveness of the workout, or it is too high, developing psychological barriers for the runners.

The athlete should never be told what the number will be, simply because no one knows before the workout begins how much running the athlete is capable of doing on that day, at that time. The posted workout should include on the *distance*, the *speed*, and the *length of recovery*. The number should merely be listed as Pmax + 1.

Pmax (presumed maximum) is the number of runs the runner thinks he or she is capable of completing at pace. But Pmax is never determined until the end of the workout, when the athlete is near fatigue. As the workout progresses, the nearly fatigued athlete decides during each recovery phase whether another run at pace is possible. Of course, the coach encourages the athlete to continue repeating as often as seems practical. When the athlete feels he or she cannot complete another run at pace, Pmax has been reached.

Chart 3
Determining Heart Rate By Timing
Pulse Rate For 10 Beats

10.0 - 60	7.5 - 80	5.0 - 120
9.9 - 61	7.4 - 81	4.9 - 122
9.8 - 61	7.3 - 82	4.8 - 125
9.7 - 62	7.2 - 83	4.7 - 128
9.6 - 63	7.1 - 85	4.6 - 130
9.5 - 63	7.0 - 86	4.5 - 133
9.4 - 64	6.9 - 87	4.4 - 136
9.3 - 65	6.8 - 88	4.3 - 140
9.2 - 65	6.7 - 90	4.2 - 143
9.1 - 66	6.6 - 91	4.1 - 146
9.0 - 67	6.5 - 92	4.0 - 150
8.9 - 67	6.4 - 94	3.9 - 154
8.8 - 68	6.3 - 95	3.8 - 158
8.7 - 69	6.2 - 97	3.7 - 162
8.6 - 70	6.1 - 98	3.6 - 167
8.5 - 71	6.0 - 100	3.5 - 171
8.4 - 71	5.9 - 102	3.4 - 176
8.3 - 72	5.8 - 103	3.3 - 182
8.2 - 73	5.7 - 105	3.2 - 188
8.1 - 74	5.6 - 107	3.1 - 194
8.0 - 75	5.5 - 109	3.0 - 200
7.9 - 76	5.4 - 111	2.9 - 207
7.8 - 77	5.3 - 113	2.8 - 214
7.7 - 78	5.2 - 115	2.7 - 222
7.6 - 79	5.1 - 118	2.6 - 231

But the workout calls for Pmax + 1. The athlete must complete one additional run - not at pace, but at *top speed*. Surprisingly, the final run - the one that is in addition to the maximum number the athlete thought possible - is almost always the fastest of the day.

Physiologically and psychologically, the Pmax + I concept is of great benefit to runners. Not only do their bodies benefit from the overload principle, but they also learn they can continue running after thinking they had reached their limits of ability.

Of course, some athletes will reach Pmax before others. Do not expect everyone to finish the workout at the same time. Do expect them to finish with about the same level of fatigue. And some will try to hit some magical number of repeats (usually divisible by 10), when an odd number may be

---

Chart 4. Volume Range

880

12 x 110 - 24 x 110
6 x 220 - 12 x 220
4 x 330 - 8 x 330
3 x 440 - 6 x 440
2 x 660 - 4 x 660

Mile

24 x 110 - 48 x 110
12 x 220 - 24 x 220
8 x 330 - 16 x 330
6 x 440 - 12 x 440
4 x 660 - 8 x 660

2-Mile

24 x 220 - 48 x 220
16 x 330 - 32 x 330
12 x 440 - 24 x 440
8 x 660 - 16 x 660

Chart 5 - Daily Workout Chart

Event _____ Workout Distance _____ Date _____ Weather _____

Name   Speed 1 2 3 4 5 6 7 8 9 10 11 12 13 14 15 16 17 18 19 20 21 22 23 24

---

best for that athlete on that day. The runners must be convinced that the exact number of runs is not important; the important thing is that they have run to their absolute limit - one run beyond their own Pmax.

The volume of running logged during each workout should fall within a range of 1½ to 3 times the athlete's racing distance. The total volume of a half-miler's workout, for example, would fall between 1320 yards and 1½ miles. If the runner cannot complete 1½ times the racing distance during a progressive interval training workout, the pace is too fast. If the runner is able to complete more than 3 times the racing distance, the pace is too slow. The total workout volume in each practice session should fall within the range shown in Chart 4. If a runner is able to do more than the maximum number, then the speed of the runs should be increased for the next workout session. But the speed should never be increased so much that the minimum number cannot be accomplished.

Developing Daily Schedules

All the coach has to do to develop a variety of progressive interval training workouts is to substitute *knowns* into the *progressive interval training formula*. The posted workout for any athlete need only include the distance and the speed (Chart 5). The other two factors - length of recovery and number - are determined during the workout. The length of recovery is the time required for the heart rate to decrease to 120; the number is the athlete's Pmax + 1.

19

ACTION ANALYSIS OF VAN NELSON

Fred Wilt
Editor, "Track Technique" Magazine

Running form is as individual as fingerprints. No two athletes ever use identical form. In fact, the form of any one athlete will alter with a change in speed.

The major difference in any athlete's sprinting form as compared to his form when running at slower speeds is simply a matter of intensity. When sprinters, who race at distances up to and including 440 yards, run at speeds slower than their maximum, their form resembles that of middle distance runners. Middle distance races extend from 880 yards to and including 6 miles. When middle distance runners sprint, their form resembles that of sprinters.

Stride length of sprinters generally varies between 7 and 8½ feet, whereas the stride of middle distance runners varies between 5 and 6 feet. Stride frequency in good sprinting varies between 4½ and 5 strides per second, while cadence in middle distance running is about 3½ strides per second. The faster the running speed, the longer is the stride, and vice versa. Forward body lean in both sprinting and middle distance running is a function of acceleration, moving faster and faster. The greater the acceleration, as seen when the sprinter leaves the blocks, the greater is the forward lean required. When running at a steady speed, thus with no acceleration, there is little if any forward lean. This is true in the case of both sprinters and middle distance runners.

The foot plant for both middle distance runners and sprinters is the same — the outer edge of the ball of the foot touches the ground first, directly beneath the runner's center of gravity. This is immediately followed by the heel grounding, which momentarily places the runner's full body weight on his heels. Then the body moves forward of the foot in contact with the ground, the heel lifts, and finally the toes leave the ground well behind the runner's center of gravity.

The stride of any runner may be divided into the recovery, supporting, and driving phases. Illustrations 1 through 10 show Van Nelson's stride.

The recovery phase begins as the toe of the foot behind the runner's body breaks contact with the ground. Illustrations 1 and 6 show Van Nelson just prior to the start of the recovery phase in his stride. The knee of the opposite leg will reach its highest point the instant the toe of this foot leaves the ground. The recovery phase for each leg ends the instant the foot touches the track beneath the runner's projected center of gravity. Illustration 4 shows Nelson's left foot grounding to conclude the recovery phase of his particular stride. Notice that both of his legs recover simultaneously. (Illustrations 2, 3, 7, and 8). Sprinters have both feet off the ground simultaneously about 60 per cent of the time during the recovery phase. Middle distance runners, however, have both feet in the air simultaneously about 50 per cent of the time during this phase.

A very brief supporting phase begins the instant the foot touches the track beneath the runner's projected center of gravity at the conclusion of the recovery phase, and ends when the center of gravity has passed forward of the foot. Illustration 9 shows Nelson just prior to the conclusion of the supporting phase. Notice his right knee is bent. Within limits, the faster the runner's speed, the more bend there is in the knee during this phase of the stride. The conclusion of the supporting phase marks the beginning of the driving phase of each stride. It is during this phase that the body is accelerated forward by extension of the levers at the hip, knee, ankle, and toe, in that order, thrusting behind the body's center of gravity. Running is a pushing action, never a pulling action. Runners should have the sensation of pushing the ground backward, away from them, during the driving phase. Nelson is shown during the driving phase in Illustrations 1, 5, 6, and 10. Middle distance runners are in contact with the track about 50 per cent of the time, while sprinters are in contact with the ground only 40 percent of the time during the driving phase.

Notice the high position of the heel of Nelson's recovery foot in Illustrations 5, 9, and 10. This is correct, and actually the faster the running speed, the higher the heels will kick up behind toward the buttocks in the recovery phase of each stride.

Nelson's true body angle can be seen in Illustrations 4, 5, 9, and 10. Using the light poles in the background as reference points, it is obvious Nelson has little if any forward lean, and his body carriage is nearly erect. This is entirely correct when running at a steady pace, not accelerating.

The eccentric, off-center thrust of each leg during the driving phase of

114

115

each stride, coupled with the lifting of the knee of the opposite leg, sets up horizontal rotations in the body which require an equal and opposite reaction. Notice the clockwise rotation of Nelson's hips in a horizontal plane, developed during the driving phase, in Illustrations 1 through 4. The equal and opposite reaction can be seen in Nelson's arms and shoulders in a counterclockwise horizontal plane in the same illustrations. The opposite is shown in Illustrations 6, 7, and 8.

As a result of these twisting actions and reactions in a horizontal plane, notice that Nelson's opposite arm follows correctly the opposite leg throughout this picture sequence.

Nelson's training, directed by Bob Tracy, St. Cloud's excellent track coach, is correct, severe, simple, and effective. He accounts for his aerobic (with oxygen) endurance needs with a continuous 10-mile run on the roads each morning at a reasonably fast pace. His anaerobic (without oxygen) endurance is acquired by daily afternoon workouts totaling approximately 10 miles each, consisting of warm-up and warm-down jogging, fast 220- and 330- yard runs, and recovery jogging following each fast run. Quite obviously the racing fortune of this champion has not been left to chance. He has earned his success through rigorous, persistent, correct daily training and an aggressive, competitive attitude.

20

INTERVAL TRAINING THROUGH USE OF THE SET SYSTEM

George R. Colfer
Dean Junior College

Interval training became a popular training method for running events in the early 50's. It actually originated in Europe in 1920 and in 1930 was adapted to Swedish conditions at which time it became known as the Fartlek or speed play method. After World War II, Emil Zatopek, using intense training known as the Zatopek method, inspired through his success the advent of what we now know as interval training. Since this time there has been an unending controversy about the pros and cons of this method. Perhaps there is no type of training that has been the target for more use and abuse than interval training. Regardless of one's opinion, most coaches, in training for the running events, use some form of interval workouts in their program. In a recent survey of successful collegiate cross-country coaches, interval training ranked second to long distance runs as the method the coaches used most in training their runners.

A general definition of interval training is a period of work or exercise followed by a prescribed recovery interval. Application of this definition to the running events implies a measured run with a measured recovery. There are several ways or techniques that may be used in planning interval training workouts. These are generally organized according to the following basic varieties:

- Distance or duration of the run.
- Speed or intensity of the run.
- Number of repetitions of the run.
- The length or duration of the recovery interval.
- Nature or type of the recovery interval.
- The frequency of the interval training sessions.

It is no secret that the success of the runners will depend on the coach's ability to combine these variables in planning the interval workout.

Benefits of Interval Training

When employed wisely, interval training offers many diverse benefits to the runner. These are aimed mainly at bettering meet performances, but also enable the athlete to accelerate more rapidly towards his potential.

- Interval training provides more work with less awareness of fatigue.
- More of a challenge is provided for the athlete.
- Quality over quantity work is emphasized.
- Competitive conditions are stimulated.
- Interval training permits rapid progress. Goals are more accurately planned and measured.
- A personal approach to training is followed.
- This method of training requires less time and space. While running at faster rates, more work can be accomplished in shorter periods of time.
- Flexibility in training is allowed. Workouts can be changed quickly if needed. A well-planned program will prevent overfatigue as a result of training.
- It is more beneficial to speed and anaerobic development.
- Aerobic benefits and heart stroke volume may be gained in a shorter period of time.
- The recovery interval avoids excessive accomulation of fatigue products in the circulatory and cardiovascular systems.
- A great deal of the research supports the theory that a proper work-recovery ratio is important to successful training.

Abuse of Interval Training

Most of the abuse in interval training is caused by human error and the lack of knowledge about the use of this method. It is not a total program, but one of various methods to be incorporated into a running program at selected times. Poor planning, lack of suitability for the individuals being trained, and poor understanding of interval training principles have developed many of the following disadvantages or weaknesses of the methods.

- Races are not run in parts. Interval times do not always indicate a mastery of the total race.

- Recovery intervals are frequently prolonged by the athlete or coach.
- This destroys the work-recovery ratio principle.
- There are limits of work and tolerance. Interval training may try to surpass them too soon.
- There is a tendency to use distance not pertinent to the event.
- Interval training should not be used until a firm foundation of aeorbic training is completed.
- There is a possibility of causing over fatigue by attempting too strenuous a program too soon. This can cause extreme setbacks in training goals. Overwork or excessive fatigue will make the athlete more susceptible to physical injury such as strains, pulls, etc.
- There is a danger of mental fatigue or stress. Interval training involves competition versus the clock. Sometimes the results or analysis can be defeating to the athlete.
- Through prolonged or excessive use, boredom or monotony can develop. The athlete may lose motivation in his training.

Most of the disadvantages stated can be overcome or need not occur if the program is well planned with the proper combination of interval training techniques and variables which can provide the athlete with the benefits of interval training while offering control over the disadvantages.

The Set System

The use of sets for interval training has several advantages over other techniques. There is greater consistency in the work performed and the measurement or analysis of the work is quite simple. Sets shorten the training time as well as make the workouts seem faster and easier to the athlete. Since consistency of the times of the runs is most important, there is less pressure or stress to record great times in practice. The challenge of the set to the runner is: Is he able to repeat the designated workout pace for each interval run of the set? In other words, can he post consistent times? Proper results require serious planning by the coach as well as knowledge of the individual abilities of his runners. Athletes in the same events can work the set together even if their workout paces are different. Competition should not be emphasized except to maintain consistency of the workout pace.

Another objective of the set system is to allow the runner to work towards his goal pace as quickly as possible. For example, if a 4:20 miler (440 goal pace = 62 seconds) has a goal of a 4:08 mile (440 goal pace = 62 seconds) his workout pace for a set of 440's should be lower than 65 seconds, which will enable him to practice closer to his goal pace. Improvement will only occur when the quality or intensity of the work is increased or the recovery interval is decreased.

To plan a specific workout using sets, the components of the set must be analyzed. Each set should consist of the following:

- A designated number of runs.
- A designated distance for each run within the set.
- A timed recovery interval, which should be adhered to strictly.
- A designated workout pace for each run within the set.
- A rest period following the completion of the set.

Types of Sets

The most efficient type of set is that of repetition of the same running distance within the set. An example would be 4 x 440. The advantage of repetition running is in establishing consistency in the pace. The ladder set would mix different distances in the same set. An example would be 2 x 330, 2 x 440, and 2 x 660. The ladder offers variation in training and in some cases will allow a more flexible approach to interval training. It should be mentioned that in a ladder set, each distance run should be repeated at least once to offer some consistency in the analysis of the work.

Number of Sets

Due to different stages of training and individual differences in ability, it is not possible to say exactly how many sets should be included in a workout. This must be the coach's decision in planning the workout. Sets may be combined using those of the same distance, of different distances or the ladder type to fit the needs of the training program. An example would be 3 sets to the workout in which set 1 is 4 x 440, set 2, 4 x 330, and set 3, 6 x 150.

After completion of the last run of a set, there should be a rest period of two to five minutes before moving on to another set or a different phase of the workout. Runners should walk during the rest period. Its length will depend upon the intensity of the workout.

Number of Runs Within a Set

A set should consist of no less than three runs and a maximum of eight. Since their training is intense, over-fatigue should be avoided. It would be more beneficial to increase the number of sets rather than surpass the maximum number of runs for a set. Runs of shorter duration would tend to be used in greater numbers. Using this concept, the quality of the training would not be affected. The distance of the event for which the training is being used should also be considered.

Distance for the Set System

While almost any distance can technically be put into a set, the quality of the work desired can best be obtained if the runs are kept to a maximum of 660 yards. The distance selected should depend largely on the events for which the training is planned. The 440 is a popular interval distance for the middle and long distance events, while 330's, 220's, and 150's are used for the shorter events. The most common distances used for the set system are: 660 yards, 600 yards, 550 yards, 440 yards, 440 yards, 352 yards, 330 yards, 300 yards, 220 yards, 150 yards, and 110 yards. The total duration of the run for set intervals should not exceed 120 seconds at longer distances and preferably 90 seconds as the runner's condition improves.

Recovery Intervals

It is important to emphasize again that the designated recovery interval should not be extended. If an athlete is not able to post consistent times, the workout pace should be lessened, not the recovery interval increased. The maximum recovery for any run should not exceed 90 seconds, while the minimum should be no less than 30 seconds. Deciding upon starting recovery lengths will depend on the condition and ability of the runner. As a rule, it would be better to start at maximums and decrease as the runner's status changes. The maximum recovery intervals are recommended for the following distances:

LENGTH OF RUN	MAXIMUM RECOVERY LENGTH
660 yards	90 seconds
600 yards	90 seconds
550 yards	90 seconds
440 yards	90 seconds
400 yards	75 seconds
352 yards	75 seconds
330 yards	75 seconds
330 yards	60 seconds
220 yards	60 seconds
150 yards	60 seconds
110 yards	60 seconds

While some recovery intervals do not allow much time, it is best if the runner keeps himself mildly active during the pause.

Workout Pace (Speed of the Run)

The pace should be established depending upon the ability and condition of the athlete. It should be realistic and attainable. As the status of the runner changes, the pace should be adjusted. In most instances, the pace for a set interval run should be faster than that of the same distance during a continuous run. A good method for checking the physiological effects of the run is to check the pulse rate of the runner at the end of the recovery interval. If the pulse rate exceeds 140, the workout pace should be lessened. This adjustment is effective in the case of beginning runners and during early season training. However, in advanced runners an allowance should be made for individual differences: therefore, this should not be an absolute rule.

Planning the Set

Through the use of the basic variables of interval training, the accompanying chart shows the different methods of planning a set workout. These methods can apply to a single set or a combination of sets. Proper planning of each set will allow for individual differences in ability as well as adding variety and flexibility to the training. The athlete should be able to work toward his goal at a faster rate of progress and with less chance of mental fatigue.

There is no definite order or progression. Combinations other than those given can be used; however, it is not advisable to change too many variables at any one time. Best results are usually obtained by a single change. Crash programs should be avoided.

Example

Starting Method. A runner begins with two sets of 4 x 440 with a workout pace of 65 seconds and a recovery length of 90 seconds.

When planning a change in this workout as progress demands, the coach may use one of the following:

Method 1. The distance, speed, number of runs, and the recovery length remain the same. The number of sets would be increased.

Method 2. The distance, speed, recovery length, and number of sets remain the same. The number of runs would be increased for each set.

Method 3. The distance of each run would be increased for each set. The speed, number of runs, recovery length, and number of sets remain the same.

Method 4. The distance, number of runs, recovery length, and number of sets would remain the same. The speed of each run would be increased.

Method 5. The distance, speed, number of runs, and number of sets remain the same. The time of the recovery length would be decreased.

Method 6. The distance would be decreased, while the speed of each run is increased. The number of runs, recovery length, and number of sets remain the same.

Method 7. The distance, number of runs, and number of sets remain the same. The speed of the runs would be increased and the recovery length is decreased. This method would produce the greatest change in the intensity of the workout.

In conclusion, it is apparent that the success of the set system depends upon the ability of the coach in organizing the training program. A review of the important factors that must be taken into consideration are:

The limiting factor for aerobic endurance tasks is the amount of oxygen intake that an athlete can accomplish in a unit of time.

- An adequate knowledge of interval training.
- A preliminary period of aerobic training.
- The integration of interval training into the total program.
- Planning of the set workout a) emphasizing quality over quantity work: b) suiting the training to the ability level of the athlete; c) use of the analysis of the training; d) patience in reaching goals and training levels; and e) making the workouts pertinent to the events for which the training is used.

METHODS	DISTANCE	SPEED	NUMBER OF RUNS PER SET	RECOVERY LENGTH	NUMBER OF SETS
STARTING METHOD	SAME	SAME	SAME	SAME	SAME
1	SAME	SAME	SAME	SAME	INCREASE
2	SAME	SAME	INCREASE	SAME	SAME
3	INCREASE	SAME	SAME	SAME	SAME
4	SAME	INCREASE	SAME	SAME	SAME
5	SAME	SAME	SAME	DECREASE	SAME
6	DECREASE	INCREASE	SAME	SAME	SAME
7	SAME	INCREASE	SAME	DECREASE	SAME

21

THE AMERICAN TECHNIQUE OF DISTANCE TRAINING

Thomas P. Rosandich,
University of Wisconsin

American distance runners have been a dominant force (except at altitude on the world scene for the past decade. Hence, the question immediately is how do they train, what is the method or technique? It is a combination and blending of many methods including those devised by Homer, Gerschler, Igloi, Stamfl, Cerutty, Lydiard, and Bowerman. Their methods were molded artistically by a variety of coaches to prepare the American athlete psychologically and physiologically for world class performances within the framework of the American society and school system.

The American technique of training evolves around the American school system, school year, and coaching scheme. Nowhere in the world is there a program comparable to the American high school and college system of sports. Thousands of coaches and hundreds of thousands of athletes come from this system and training techniques that are uniquely our own, yet based on the best parts of many foreign systems in the same way that our physical education program throughout America was adopted in part from the German Turners and the Czech Falcons. Circuit training which is widely used in America originated in England.

Probably the biggest changes made by American coaches have been in their methods of application in recent years. Often in the past, coaches established a training program of blind obedience requiring stern discipline which can never be a wholesome substitute for the word *respect*. Unfortunately, in this process the reasons for training were never understood and often beginning athletes suffered discomfort, pain, and agony without understanding that this was an essential part of training experienced by all athletes. Only too often these athletes left the program in fear of what was to come next, fear of the unknown, fear of being hurt, and fear of failure.

These fears should be attacked immediately by the coach. He must communicate with the athlete and provide him with the understanding of what training is all about, what he is to do, and why he is to do it. Thus, the coach, i.e. teacher, must and should be able to explain logically and in layman's terms the physiological principles of training. The coach then, as an artist, should be able to style and apply these principles psychologically to the athlete in the form of a routine and pattern that has the probability of success. A coach should give the team a written examination on the training program to see if he is communicating.

Physiological Principles of Training

In order for an athlete to perform a work load, he must be able to change glycogen in the muscle tissue into energy, and to do this, he must have an adequate supply of oxygen.

In order for an athlete to perform a given work load, he must have an adequate supply of oxygen.

Aerobic (meaning with oxygen) metabolism of glycogen occurs when sufficient oxygen is available to meet the need during the given rate of work. To be able to withstand fatigue during this rate of work is to have aerobic endurance. It becomes apparent that the limiting factor for general or aerobic endurance is the amount of oxygen intake that an athlete can accomplish in a unit of time, since he cannot store oxygen. Jim Ryun has recorded the highest oxygen consumption efficiency value ever (82.9 per cent).

The human body at rest requires between 200 and 300 cubic centimeters of oxygen per minute, and this amount can increase 20 times during vigorous muscular activity. Peter Snell, New Zealand's great miler, recorded an oxygen intake of 5.502 liters per minute.

Oxygen intake is determined by the following factors: the intensity of the work; the ventilation of the lungs which increases proportionately to the amount of work; the oxygen carrying capacity of the blood, which is limited by the number of red blood cells and the hemoglobin content of the red corpuscles; the efficiency of the performance; and the minute volume of the heart.

A work level which is constant or steady is performed aerobically and can often continue for an indefinite period of time. In certain athletic events such as the 440, the requirement for energy in class performance is so great in a short period of time that the body cannot meet the demands for oxygen with which to metabolize glycogen. In instances such as this, the body metabolizes glycogen anaerobically, or without oxygen. Anaerobic work is 50 per cent less efficient due to the build-up of lactic acid in the cells and blood. Lactic acid lowers the pH level (degree of acidity-alkalinity) of the blood.

During such a state the deficit in oxygen intake creates an oxygen debt. This debt must be repaid during the recovery following the exercise. We witness this repayment by the continued deep breathing and relatively high pulse rate following the exercise. The limit of work capabilities of an athlete is then the sum of two factors: first, the level of maximum oxygen intake per unit of time; and second, the amount of oxygen debt that the individual can contract.

A simple application of the previously mentioned principles would be to introduce the athlete to the Harvard Step Test so that each individual athlete could learn to evaluate his own progress during any stage of his training. We cannot emphasize enough the understanding and using of pulse levels in training because they are the key to the total method of distance training explained in this article. Furthermore, it provides even the layman with an elementary understanding of the physiological principles involved in training. This alone can provide any athlete with a great deal of confidence instead of fear of the unknown and discomforts.

The evaluations and feelings should be recorded in a daily training diary. We feel the diary is a vital tool in the overall training program of any athlete but it is useless unless it shows a trend in training. A training diary should not merely be a series of spaces and squares and checks but rather a sum total of feelings and attitudes of an athlete after a particular workout, his reaction to a work load, his pulse, his temperature, the surface he trains on, the temperature, and most important, his feelings - good or bad, relaxed or sore. An athlete should also write a weekly summary in his diary which forces him to reflect upon what he did and where he is going. What is so unfortunate in America is our over-commitment to competition with two or three meets a week rather than seven days of training and pointing towards specific targets and goals. Mid-week meets should be approached only as workouts to be of any value over the long haul.

The Five Steps In The American Method

The American training method is a progression of five steps which reflect the theories and concepts of the greatest coaches in the field and are applied to the American school system and sport season. The method, in essence, is a two-a-day workout, 365 days a year; a method where volume is replaced by quality after a sound base has been established.

Dr. Jim Counsilman, the swimming coach from Indiana, diagramed these five steps to estimate the relative benefits of these two variables - cardiovascular endurance and strength or speed. We believe the accompanying diagram reflects a good picture of these two variables, although there is a slight tendency to underrate strength in the marathon and fartlek portions of the program. It is obvious that marathon training offers little to the sprinter other than basic conditioning which would permit him to do more repetitions in a given workout.

This method has been used effectively by Bill Bowerman of Oregon and Bob Lawson at Iowa State.

Marathon Training

Marathon or volume training is slow, continuous running at relatively low speed over distances up to 30 miles. The heart and lung rate during these slow, steady runs will approach 150 beats per minute. Because of the nature of the type of training, little stimulus is offered to the development of strength of the muscles of the legs, nor does it greatly stimulate the heart. However, Swedish research indicates that this type of training provides the best method of improving the capillary system. Hence it improves aerobic endurance.

Secondly, this type of training is invaluable in preparing the body properly to avoid needless injury of muscles and connective fibers. It provides the necessary base for future work. Marathon training is best done in the summer and it can be worked into many of the road races that take place at that time of the year.

The American Method

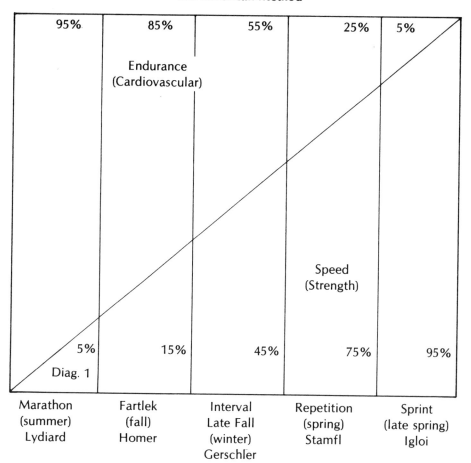

95%	85%	55%	25%	5%
	Endurance (Cardiovascular)			
			Speed (Strength)	
5%	15%	45%	75%	95%

Diag. 1

Marathon (summer) Lydiard	Fartlek (fall) Homer	Interval Late Fall (winter) Gerschler	Repetition (spring) Stamfl	Sprint (late spring) Igloi

Fartlek Training

Fartlek or speed play originated in Sweden and is probably one of the most misused methods of training in America. It is characterized by a long run over undulating terrain which is broken into a series of slow jogs and fast sprints and interlaced with a series of gymnastics. This training method requires tremendous mental discipline by the participants in order to be executed properly. Since it is often done in the forest, it is away from the control of the coach unless he is clever enough to be in the forest at the trail junctions and gymnastic stations.

At the conclusion of a proper fartlek, the athlete should be in a state of exhaustion from a self-sustained push. The sauna at this moment is probably the answer to exhilerated recovery. A key phrase in fartlek training may be, *The mind controls the body.* An example of application would be when the muscles first begin to tighten before exhaustion, the athlete must think relaxation - speed - relaxation. The mind must concentrate on the task of running and technique and not on how one feels.

Fartlek running courses should include hills - long ones if possible, up to 500 yards - which the runner can attack with vigor as a sprinter. To perform this type of training, the base of marathon training is needed especially to continue the drive on hills, over the crest to a point beyoon what has been achieved before, even if the pace drops. Relaxation again is the key.

A reminder to help with relaxation of the lower back and upper torso is to exhale slowly and deliberately in a forced method in an effort to rid the body of carbon dioxide. Next, the athlete should inhale deeply and deliberately to give a psychological and physiological lift to fill the lungs with nourishing oxygen which is necessary for oxidizing the glucose. This is mind over matter.

In addition to the freedom of playing in the forest, which stimulates an athlete to greater work loads, a forgotton factor in fartlek is changing stride, which is forced by the variance in terrain. These changes in stride aid the runner in adjusting to all types of challenges that he might need in competition and at the same time aid in the development of all muscle groups used in running. In addition, the natural roll of the ground and the foot with it is a vital factor in stretching the muscle sheath to avoid shin splints. The Germans have recently completed research designed to prevent shin splints. They devised a method of taking the foot in the hands in a sitting position and forcing it in hyperextensions and rotations in all directions. This we have called the *Tucker twist.*

When the athlete cannot maintain the running load or bursts of sprints, he should stop for gymnastics or calisthenics. However, these are rhythm gymnastics of swinging, twisting, bending, stretching exercises, done as the athlete bounces and hops in a forest clearing. Hip-swinging or race-walking drills tied together with twisting exercises will rid the body of gas pockets.

Dispersed throughout the forest can be log stations for resistance work. These are wooden logs cut to various lengths for one-, two-, and four-man drills. Thus an athlete has an opportunity to use a different set of muscles, and at the same time he is receiving total body conditioning which is the prime objective of fartlek training.

Fartlek training takes place in the fall to coincide with the cross-country season. As mentioned previously, it prepares the total body physically for an increased tempo of work. In many ways it is similar to the hill work that Lydiard talks about in his marathon training. Dr. Gerschler's main criticism of this method is what he called the lack of scientific control or pace work, although he had a healthy respect for Homer's fartlek training.

Interval Training

Interval or pace training, controlled by the pulse rate and the coach over set distances, is probably the heart of all training programs for virtually all sports, in one form or another. Unfortunately, next to fartlek training, this is one of the most confused and abused methods used by American coaches.

The key to interval training is the pulse rate durng the recovery period or rest interval, which should never excede more than 90 seconds. Any time that the athlete takes more than a 90-second interval, he is no longer engaging in interval training but rather in repetition training.

Let us establish a guide for pulse rate control training. For maximum development of the heart, the pulse rate must reach at least 180 beats per minute. This can be achieved readily over a distance of 220 yards which is often considered to be the perfect distance for interval training. It should be noted that the heart stretches in the first 30 seconds after exercise ceases, not during the period of work. The need for more oxygen causes the heart to pump up. This pumping up action stretches the heart. The more times that this can be repeated, the more efficient the heart becomes, thus causing the pulse rate to drop - this is conditioning.

During the rest interval, the athlete should wait until the pulse returns to 120 beats per minute before starting his next repetition. By the same token, this rest period should not excede 90 seconds. At 120 beats the capillaries begin to close down so that he needs added stress of more repeats to create this 180 pulse rate for repeated heart stretch. The minimum recovery period should be at least 30 seconds so that the heart can use this interval for heart stretch.

If the heart rate has not recovered to 120 to 130 in 90 seconds, the exercise has either been too violent in tempo or too long. Thus, these are the controlling factors in establishing training loads and patterns.

There are four variables in interval training with an infinite number of workout routines possible. An aid to remember these variables is the word DIRT.

D - indicates the distance to be run during the workout.

I - stands for interval, or the length of rest between each repetition. Indicate whether it is sitting, lying, walking or jogging.

R - points out the number of repetitions in the workout, or sets of repetitions.

T - indicates the time or pace each repetition is run in.

An example of an interval workout for a 4:20 miler might be determined in the following manner.

Example A	Example B
D - 440	Distance plus - Increase
I - 1 minute - Jog	Interval minus - Decrease
R - 16 - 20	Repetition plus - Increase
T - 69 seconds	Time Minus - Decrease

The following rules can help a coach apply the principles of interval training. It is obvious why an athlete should have a good knowledge of the Harvard Step Test and pulse control and how the diary can become a vital tool in any training program.

1. Change the rest interval first. Again, this interval should be somewhere between 30 and 90 seconds.

2. Next, change the repetition or number of runs.

3. Increase the length of each repetition - anywhere from 100 to 400 yards. Distances over 400 yards are not recommended.

4. Once the distances increase, go back to the original pattern of rest and repetition.

5. As he progresses, the athlete must recover in 90 seconds or less.

If he cannot recover, the workout is too tough and it should be stopped for that day and revised accordingly. The coach and athlete should review the athlete's diary and pattern to search out the point where the program is failing him. It could be his execution, emotion, nervousness, injury, fatigue or even illness.

Interval training is the most scientific of the training methods. The coach has a controlled situation before him where the athlete is paced at all times. This portion of training in the American system runs well from late fall or the cross-country championships into the indoor season and early spring, where it is superseded by repetition training or quality work, i.e. speed.

Repetition Training

This is a modern method of training that is too often mistaken for interval training. The main difference here is that the interval or rest is controlled by the athletes; and secondly, the distances that are run are often longer than those used in interval work.

If the rest interval is over 90 seconds, it is repetition training. In reality, the athlete rests until he is fully recovered for his next repeat. The distances that are run are often up to three-quarters of the racing distance. Finally, the pace at which the work is done is usually faster than race pace.

If the speed of the repetition run is maintained at a fast pace, it is believe the benefit will be the development of anaerobic endurance since a large oxygen debt is contracted during this type of running. The 4:20 miler might attempt a repetition workout similar to the following: 2 x 4 x ¾ mile in average racing pace plus 3 to 4 seconds per quarter; or in this instance, 68 to

69 seconds x 3 (quarters) or 3.24 to 3:27 for each repetition of the three-quarter mile. A walk to almost complete recovery should follow each repetition. The length of the rest interval may increase as the workout proceeds.

Two other terms associated with this method of training are quality and super-quality training. Quality training is when the athlete is working at race pace or slightly faster. Super-quality, as coined by Lawson of Iowa State, is done at 90 per cent effort or faster. In other words, it is an all-out run with concentration on relaxation and technique. These types of training are governed by effort, not by a set number of repetitions to be run in a given workout. When a runner fails to run two or three efforts at race pace or faster, then he should decrease the distance at which he is working and attempt to reach race pace again. If this cannot be achieved, he should stop for the day. This is called a regressive type of workout: 660 - 550 - 440 - 330 - 220 - 110.

This type of workout would be predominant during the middle of the outdoor competitive season, as the coach is preparing for the ultimate in training, i.e. sprint speed. We might mention that throughout all steps of this program resistance work plays a vital role, even during the height of the competitive season.

Sprint or Speed Training

Sprinting will create irritation in the system, or discomfort to the athlete. Again, he must learn to understand and recognize these discomforts of running so that he can go through the barrier.

In all sprinting, rhythm must be stressed in all drills and exercises in an effort to achieve complete relaxation during maximum effort. When this is achieved, the coach has a champion.

Sprint training may take several forms but to run fast the athlete must educate his nervous system to factors which require spontaneous reaction. The physiological effects of different sprint routines vary. Interval sprinting, for instance, is a method of alternating sprinting from 25 to 110 yards with a jog of an equal distance between each sprint. In this routine, fatigue will inhibit the runner from top speed after a few repetitions. This type of workout is mainly aerobic.

Acceleration sprinting is characterized by a gradual increase in speed from jogging to top speed. This type of training is particularly valuable during cold weather. Remember, an athlete should be completely warmed up and perspiring before he sprints or he may experience headaches, nausea or injury. An accelerated sprint could be easy jogging for 110, and easing off into a recovery walk for 110.

A formula for stating pace can be found by timing 110 at maximum effort. This time is then multiplied by 2 and 5 seconds are added. An example could be 110 in 13.5 x 2 + 5 for a 33.0 over 220 yards.

Quality training is where the athlete is working at race pace or slightly faster.

With pace established, a weekly training pattern can be formed which could be as follows: first day overdistance; second speed; third pace; fourth speed; fifth pace or workout of choice; sixth quality trials or meet; seventh long run.

If the athlete cannot run short intervals in his speed training, then he will not be able to run the total distance in his race in class time. The key to sprint training is a solid base established in steps one and two before quality or speed work is attempted. The athlete must work constantly on relaxation at high speed. This is not a natural skill - it comes only with constant repetition and continuous thought. A coach cannot yell *relax* and expect relaxation from an athlete - the opposite will probably occur.

The essence of all training can be summed up with the five S's or achieved through the five-step pattern outlined in this article. They are stamina, strength, speed, suppleness, and self-confidence.

These five ingredients can be achieved in a logical fashion via the American method presented. All that is required is continuous, intelligent, and progressive hard work.

22

MILE MECHANICS AND TRAINING TECHNIQUES

Bill Bowerman,
University of Oregon

It has been said: *A good big man can always beat a good little man.* Most of us prefer and believe more heartily in the axiom: *It is not the size of the dog in the fight, but rather the amount of fight in the dog.* In order to develop a miler, the coach must have a man who has some ability and a great deal of determination.

At the University of Oregon it has been our good fortune to have men of the stature of Ken Reiser, national two mile and steeplechase champion; Bill Dellinger, national mile, two mile and 5,000 meter champion; Jim Bailey, national mile champion, Jim Grelle, national mile champion; and now Dyrol Burleson, AAU mile champion at the age of nineteen.

Many of our contemporaries asked us how we developed these men and some asked why. We have also asked ourselves the same questions. In attempting to arrive at some of the answers, it was our good fortune to have a Ph.D. candidate do a four-year study on our middle distance and distance runners. We are indebted to a number of coaches for their generous contributions to this study. A few of these include Holmer, for his Fartlek; Stampft, for his interval method in *On Running*; Igloi, for his indirect contributions through Dale Ranson at North Carolina; Ceruty, *On Running*; the many outstanding United States coaches with whom we have exchanged ideas - Brutus Hamilton, Hec Edmundson, Flint Hanner, Payton Jordan, Karl Schlademan, Bob Newland, and Dave Rankin to name a few.

A runner is able to maintain better balance by deep rhythmical breathing. A runner should beware of labored, panting breathing.

We feel that Oregon weather contributes to the success of our runners because it is vigorous enough to keep an athlete hustling. Adversity must be overcome in order to achieve success. The Nurmis, Elliots, Bannisters, and other great runners came from a climate similar to that found in Oregon.

The balance of this article will be devoted to a discussion of body mechanics and our training schedule. We believe body mechanics should be taught; however, if the athlete achieves better results without them, then they should be abandoned. Regarding a training schedule, it is a guide, similar to a road map, which should help a runner get from point A to point B.

Mechanics

Arm Carry. 1. A distance runner should carry his arms slightly away from his chest because this position raises the chest cage, making for a great air capacity.

2. His arms should be bent at the elbow between a 45 and 30° angle for two reason: (a) The shorter the arm swing, the shorter is the corresponding leg swing. We believe a short, quick, light stride is more economical than one which reaches ahead of the center of gravity. The long stride should be used at the end of a race, and the runner's arm should be lowered to a 60 or 45° angle: (b) Circulation is aided by position. Remember, as a youngster how one could keep water in a bucket by swinging the bucket in an arm's length circle? The blood also reacts to centrifugal force. Circulation is aided by maintaining less swing in the arms.

Breathing. Some runners naturally breathe rhythmically and easily. We will not dwell on oxygen debt other than to say we believe a better balance is maintained by deep rhythmical breathing. A runner should beware of labored, panting breathing.

Some work is done on two, three or four step rhythm. Our runners walk and count breathe in one, two; out one, two; and then try the three and four count rhythm. Most of them have found the most effective rhythm to be the three count.

We believe a runner's mouth should be slightly open and most of his breathing should be done through his mouth

Foot Landing. We believe it was Aramas Valste, the Finnish coach, who said, *European sprinters sprint like runners; American runners run like sprinters.* At that time the American runners were running distances of 1500 meters and longer on the balls of their feet.

Our runners are told to experiment with the flat-foot landing, the heel-to-ball landing, and the ball-to-heel landing. Eventually, they will use the type or types of landings that best suit their needs. We have had outstanding runners use each of these foot techniques. Ken Reiser had a very efficient flat landing. Jim Bailey used the ball-to-heel landing, and Bill Dellinger uses a heel-to-ball landing most of the time.

A distance runner should carry his arms slightly away from his chest because this position raises the chest cage, making for a greater air capacity.

Training Schedule

A good banker, lawyer or doctor is constantly practicing his profession. How can a runner become proficient if he devotes only March, April, and May to his development?

We prepare a master schedule which starts in October and extends through June. Let us assume that Burleson and Grelle want to run the mile in four minutes in June. We prepare a master schedule which shows 75-second quarters in October; November 72's; December 69's; January 67's; February 65's; March 63's; April 62's; May 61's; and June 60's.

The training guide will be made up each month so the runner will practice interval pace work at the objective pace with a test or competitive effort every ten days to two weeks. The mile in mid-October is run in five minutes. Should the runner fail to achieve his fine-minute mile, he would go into the next training period at the old pace effort.

What distances and what rest interval do we use? Each monthly training period is started with distances of 660, 440, 220 or 110 yards with rest intervals the same distance as the distance run. The second week the rest interval is cut to one-half the running distance. The third and fourth weeks the rest interval is one-quarter the distance run. At the start of a new month and reduced time, the rest interval returns to the distance run.

How often to our runners practice various fundamentals? We believe there should be two or three hard days a week, with light work on alternate days. The hard work should be either two days of interval and one of Fartlek, or two of Fartlek and one of interval running.

23

DEVELOPING A FINISHING KICK IN MIDDLE DISTANCE RUNNERS

Kenneth L. O'Brien,
University of Massachusetts

How often have track coaches heard a runner say: "I could have won that race if I had a kick", or " I could have caught him if I had started my kick sooner." Statement similar to these are made by international competitors as well as high school point scorers. They are referring to a most important attribute of a middle distance or distance runner which often means the difference between a highly satisfying or an extremely discouraging performance.

A finishing kick is the ability of a runner to activate his physiological and psychological reserve to increase, or in some cases merely sustain, his speed over the final portion of the race. Middle distance events, the 600, 880, and 1000 yard runs, lie between the sprint of the 440 and the controlled pace, and then the sprint of the mile. Acquisition of a finishing kick is difficult to learn and adequate work to insure proper development is too often neglected. However, we are convinced that this ability is the most important requirement for a successful middle distance competitor. To develop successful runners in these events, a coach must consciously provide a progressive and planned training program which emphasizes the learning of this skill.

A training program for all running events should be both general and specific. The general training procedures are varied, usually emphasized during the pre-season practices, and are aimed at developing a basic level of condition. Specific training practices are emphasized during the competitive season and relate to the skill or technique involved in the event. Sprint and hurdle training are obvious examples of this concept. General conditioning for these events consists of body exercises, weight-lifting, distance running, and interval work. Specific or skill training encompasses starting and finishing technique, hurdling form, baton passing, and repetitions at racing pace for neuromuscular coordination. Specialized skills are evident in these running events; consequently, they should be practiced diligently.

Too often training for middle distance runners is merely a general conditioning program. Some pace work represents an inadequate attempt at specific training. Coaches and runners do not view a finishing kick as a specialized skill, similar to starting technique, and as important to race success in middle distance running as starts are to sprinting. In order to develop this skill, we found that a concentrated effort applied in an organized training program produces convincing results.

As mentioned previously, a finishing kick is a physiological and psychological effort in the final stages of a race. To develop a kick, coaches and runners must attempt to improve both of these aspects in a runner. Progressive work will automatically improve the physical condition; however, the coach must work diligently to develop the necessary psychological readiness. Personal conversation with each runner before and after pactice, during rest intervals or while he is running, should attempt to relate the purpose of each drill and the relevance of each phase of practice to the final goal. The three most important attitudes to stress in middle distance running are confidence, a feeling of personal and race control, and aggressiveness. If they are worked on long enough, control and aggressiveness can almost become habits, and confidence abounds when these habits meet with favorable results in practice or in competition.

In each instance, our discussion deal first with the basic concepts of middle distance running which should be considered as specific skill, and is followed by suggested training methods to use in developing these skills.

Running Rhythm

Concept: Develop a rhythm of running for each individual so that the stride length and stride rate are relaxing and not physically demanding. In middle distance running, the greatest danger lies in inefficient overstriding and the bounding action commonly associated with long-legged novice runners. The stride rate, or tempo, should be crisp throughout the race. Stride length differs during the race. In the first half to three-quarters of the race, the reach of the lead (front) leg and the extension of the drive (rear) leg is not at full effort and the runner develops a feeling of running within himself. The runner's stride is not choppy; however, there is sub-maximal muscular effort involved with plenty of push and reach available if he is called upon for a final burst.

Method A: The coach should remind the runners verbally of their stride rhythm during the initial training stages by calling a rhythmic count or

In middle distance running, the stride rate, or tempo, should be crisp throughout the race.

beating on a can or drum if their tempo varies. Suggest that each individual listen to the sound of his feet contacting the track and count his own tempo.

Method B: Carry the concept of sub-maximal effort of the legs into the breathing effort. By employing inhalation well within the maximum, and utilizing forced exhalation on every other downbeat of the running tempo, the middle distance runner coordinates his upper and lower body into one efficient rhythmic mechanism operating well in check.

Method C: Numerous repetitions at a slow pace over distances of 110 to 440 yards during pre-season practice will develop the ability to relax at running tempo. To build a feeling of control over oneself and comfort in the initial stages of the race leads to confidence in the ability to meet the challenges of the final surge with the effort which has been kept in reserve.

Running Position

Concept: The second concept is easy to teach; however, it is a neglected skill in racing. Proper position in middle distance racing is extremely important. It decreases the possibility of falling victim to the unexpected box, keeps the actual distance covered close to the true measured distance, and insures the closest possible position to the lead when the moment for striking occurs. In light of these considerations, the most advantageous position is snugly behind the outside shoulder of the opponent. Coaches should encourage their runners to remain approximately one foot behind the opponent and placed so that the inside leg remains just outside the opponent's outside leg. This position eliminates the necessity of overcoming the one or two yards normally allowed in an attempt to avoid a rear leg kick-up when following directly behind an opponent. The necessity for this crucial delay and move to the outside when coming off the last turn often causes the finishing surge to fall short at the tape. This delay can be eliminated by proper running position.

Method A: Have the runners practice in groups of two to five during warm-up and repetition work on the track, maintaining this position as closely as possible during varied running speeds. Position running in pairs and in closely bunched groups also forces runners to concentrate on maintaining their individual running rhythm without being influenced by others in the race.

Method B: Have two teammates run repetitions around the curve and in the same lane trying to eliminate body contact and avoid stepping on lane lines. Runners should adhere so closely to their opponents that they can be seen by them, and as added intimidation, encourage them to make their controlled rhythmic breathing clearly audible to the opponent. This can cause an upsetting concern on the part of the leader, and a confident feeling of control within the pursuer. To fully appreciate the value of this seemingly insignificant skill, have the runners picture themselves running 880 yards with an opponent shadowing six inches behind them who appears to know what he is doing and is waiting to strike if they falter.

Pace Consciousness

Concept: The third concept and one of the most important skills in middle distance running is that any race can be broken into anticipated segments, and the level of training must be geared to develop pace awareness and pace tolerance commensurate with each individual's ability. We recommend the 220- and 300- yard intervals as the most valuable pace developers for middle distance runners. In any given period of training, as the season progresses, one-half of our training time is spent on the concept of developing appropriate conditioning and pace consciousness through 220- and 300-yard intervals. As an example, a 1:56 half-miler should be able to run 220's at 25 to 31 seconds on command. A 2:12 half-miler should develop this ability as approximate speeds in the range of 29 to 35 seconds. Runners should be able to run consistently prescribed 220's within .5 of a second, 440's within 1.0 seconds of the desired time, and 660's within 1.0 to 1.5 seconds.

Method A: Start the beginners with the more experienced runners who act as pacers and concentrate on mastery of varied times over one distance.

Method B. After a designated pace has been run, the runner and the coach should guess the actual elapsed time and record the guesses, with the winner to be determined by the smallest total error at the end of practice.

Method C: To adjust to the varying pace conditions of a race, run repetitions by alternate slow-fast times. For example, a 2:00 half-miler would anticipate a race of 29-31-31-29 seconds for 220 segments. He would then train at alternate slow 31, fast 29, second 220 repetitions with a short rest interval. Make a concentrated effort to impress on each runner that the slow segment is merely an extension of the rest interval and that only the 29-second 220 repetition produces effort. This gradually develops the ability of a runner to feel that while running a racing pace similar to this one he is actively resting with a running rhythm that does not require vigorous extensive thrust or powerful leg reach. In short, he is running at racing pace, but running within himself and confident that he has something in reserve. As the season progresses, slowly decrease the times of the slow and fast repetitions while increasing the number of repetitions gradually. A 2:06 half-miler can be expected to run 10 x 220 at 33-31 seconds while a half-miler running 1:54 or better will gradually progress to 14-18 x 220 alternating 28-26 second paces and a slow 110 walk rest interval. By running 16 x 220's at this pace, a runner can feel confident of running four continuous 220's at approximately resting pace.

The passing of a runner off the last turn or breaking contact with the opponents to run away from the rest of the field is the result of correct conditioning utilized in an efficient running rhythm, executing an intelligently paced racing plan, and being in the proper position at the desired moment.

All of these skills lead up to the explosive driving surge that is directly observable and thrilling to spectators and runners alike. As the moment of truth in a middle distance race approaches, the hours of physical training and verbal interaction are tested. The runner is striding rhythmically but certainly not easily, his breathing is smooth but strained and quite heavy, and he doubts whether or not he is running within himself. In order to remain confident when this feeling of control is challenged, the middle distance runner must be able to activate his feeling of aggressiveness. Due to the sustained speed of the middle distance race, the short finishing distance, and the danger of natural boxes, this is the moment when he must shift into an explosive effort as opposed to a long, gradual struggle for acceleration. This explosive and overpowering kick must be developed in order to be successful in middle distance races.

The Shift

Concept: Proper training for a finishing kick emphasizes a physical ability and mental willingness to respond to the command for all-out effort at the greatest stages of fatigue. The shift is an actual shortening of the stride length and quickening of the stride rate which creates the same effect as the gear shift of an automobile. By assuming a slight forward lean of the upper body and shortening the stride for 10 to 50 yards, the runner assumes the most beneficial position to apply added force to his body by a vigorous and full extension of the drive (rear) leg which he has knowingly held in check while running within himself. With body lean, shortened stride, and forceful extension, the momentum of the runner is increased thus allowing for an increased stride length. The greater stride length and the quickened tempo result in increased speed. The skill of shifting, and the ability, willingness, and confidence to do so is developed by utilizing the following training methods.

Method A: Leapfrogging can be used as a warm-up or conditioning technique. All middle distance men should run in single file with the last man shifting and sprinting to the front on command. Once everyone has accelerated to the front, the speed of the entire line increases and leapfrogging begins again.

Method B: Accelerating repetitions comprise one of the most beneficial training methods for developing the ability to kick explosively. Any given distance to be run is merely divided into segments and the last segment is run noticeably faster than the first. Noticeable time differences occuring over short distances of 110 to 300 yards can only be accomplished by an explosive sprinting acceleration which these drills require.

Method C: Hill cresting. This type of workout should not be attempted until eight gradually progressive hill workouts have been completed. This is the most demanding drill of the entire program and is as important as pace consciousness for middle distance success. Hill cresting is the best developer of

The three most important attitudes to stress in middle distance running are confidence, a feeling of personal and race control, and aggressiveness.

the explosive ability needed in a finishing kick and should be included as a part of a steady training diet. Locate a hill of 15 to 30 degrees and 100 to 300 yards in length. The hill is to be repeated each time by running the first third slowly and the second third at a medium pace. Fifty yards from the top the runner should lean forward, shorten his stride, and drive more forcefully with his rear leg.

Always emphasize carrying the sprint over the top and continue for 50 to 110 yards on the flat. This drill teaches the proper reaction at the point of fatigue similar to that which occurs during the race. Now it is being done against a resistance in the form of the hill. When the hill has been crested and the resistance has been overcome, the runner's legs should uncoil like springs increasing the stride length, and the powerful explosive kick is born. Only in a racing situation when the legs begin their aggressive drive and there is no resistance to overcome, can the value of the power developed through this method be fully realized.

The Finishing Drive

Concept: The body has been mobilized by a willing mind and the drive to the tape has started. Once a runner begins his kick, there can be no stopping because he has activated within the minds of his opponents the basic instinct of the chase. There is no room for both doubt and determination in his heart. Once a runner responds during the painful stages of fatigue, he must be prepared to continue his aggressive driving surge, when it hurts the most, beyond every challenge both human and natural.

Method A: Practices must be organized so that even the smallest component of the entire practice (exclusive of the warm-down) is pursued with increased effort during the heaviest fatigue. For instance, 75 Jumping Jacks as a possible warm-up exercise should be done 25 slow, 25 medium, and 25 all-out. The more opportunity there is to encourage all-out effort during fatigue, the more nearly t:is principle becomes a habit with each competitor.

Method B: The entire practice must be organized so that the last segment of the body of practice requires the greatest demand. For instance, a workout of 15 x 220 can be done 12 at a 31-second average and the final 3 at 28 seconds. A workout of 3 x 4 x 300 can be done 43, 42, 41, 40 rest 42, 41, 40, 39 rest 41, 40, 39, and 38.

Method C: For ultimate contribution combine the workouts that require acceleration power (hill cresting) with the workouts which require the greatest effort during the highest stage of fatigue. Run sets of hill repetitions over 220 and 300 yards with times decreasing. The first one-third of each segment should be equally as slow so that the decrease in time must be accomplished by the steady middle segment or by the increase in effort over the top.

Good track performances are not automatic. A well-organized practice program is essential for success, with daily, weekly, monthly, and seasonal goals as part of the plan. Work loads should be gradual and progressive and under no circumstances should an athlete attempt a new level of training until he demonstrates consistently that he can handle the work at the level in which he is currently involved. The purpose of this article is to point out the concepts of middle distance running as skills to be practiced and developed, toward building a finishing kick. It is not intended to suggest specific times and distances, but to suggest methods to mold a systematic program applicable to the ability of any middle distance runner.

With the correct general conditioning, the learning of the physiological and psychological skills of running within oneself, the accompanying feeling of race control, and the daily workouts aimed at developing the ability to supply maximum effort at the point of fatigue, middle distance runners will have the confidence and the ability to start a finishing kick that will carry them beyond the tape and well beyond marks which they may never have attained.

PART IV

THE LONG DISTANCES AND CROSS COUNTRY

24

PLANNING FOR CROSS-COUNTRY SUCCESS

Bruce L. Waha,
Redford High School, Detroit, Michigan
and
Robert Briner,
Spring Arbor College

Successful coaches realize that some of their most important work is done out of season. The fact is that to a large degree the amount and quality of pre-season planning determines how much of the team's potential is to be realized. When it comes to cross-country, this is certainly true.

The important first step in planning an upcoming cross-country season is for the coach to acquaint himself thoroughly with his personnel. He should review what he knows about each of the returning runners, and add the new things he has learned since the last cross-country season. A folder should be kept on each one for this purpose. Folders on new runners should be started as soon as the coach knows they are going to be candidates for his squad.

When we say we want to know our personnel, we mean it. We want to know about running experience, the amount of work each runner has been exposed to in the past, what type of temperament he has, his physical characteristics, how much help (or hindance) we can expect from his parents, his scholastic capabilities, etc. This may seem extreme, but we feel that distance running requires the total effort of the total person, and in order for us to do the most effective job of coaching, we must know as much about that person as possible.

Only when the team as individuals is known, can the motivational approaches we are going to make to each during the season be planned intelligently. We must know the individual in order to learn whether or not it is going to take coaxing, prodding, pushing, praise, persuasion, tact, ignoring, or any combination of these to produce maximum results in each runner. In the case of veteran runners, a review is necessary to decide where both progress and mistakes were made in motivational approaches the past season. Then plans can be made accordingly.

Two motivating procedures are used with each boy every year. The first of these is to set both short- and long-range goals. These goals are based on past performance, capability, and motivational impact. In other words, when dealing with the type of boy to whom achievement spurs greater efforts and hence more achievement, our short-range goals will be set within easy reach. The reverse is true when dealing with a boy who became complacent upon achieving a short-range goal.

The second of these procedures is to explain the various reactions to distance running which certain boys will have. We do this by explaining the accompanying chart to them as follows:

1. The quitter who hits the barrier, bounces back, retreats, and quits the squad.

2. The runner who is satisfied with mediocrity and wants to run as long as he is not expected to experience any pain or sacrifice.

3. The individual who works fairly hard and wants to be up there with the good runners, but who does not have the desire to be the best.

4. The achiever who smashes through every barrier to attain the goal. Of course, this little talk is always concluded with the question: *Which one are you going to be this year?*

We have found it helpful to make a general work load plan for the entire season. This planning is done by considering the squads work needs at various stages of the season. Naturally, the number of practice miles run in a week in which there are two meets will be less than for a week with one or no meets.

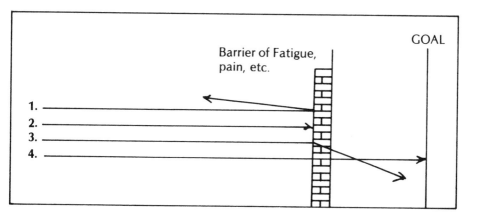

Change-of-pace work is incorporated into a variety of different drills in order to familiarize the runners with actual racing conditions. During the course of a race, a runner must change his pace several times as competition and course dictate. We want our boys to be able to change pace often and still run a paced race for the entire distance.

Time trials are used as an incentive device, a measuring device, and a monotony breaker. During the season runners are timed for 880 yards, a mile, two miles, three miles, and the total course.

At least twice a week, hill work is conducted as part of the workout. Both continuous loops and repeated climbs and descents are used.

Another thing that is incorpoated into each workout is a personal word or two with each man even if it is only, "Hello, how's it going?" We make it a point to talk to every boy. We also make it a point to speak to our runners in the halls and around campus. Coaching is to a large extent a selling job. This is especially true in cross-country where a boy is asked for so much hard physical exertion. The personal touch helps in selling the coach and his program to the runners.

Cross-country running to the uninitiated must seem to be the least complicated of athletic activities. The truth is that successful long distance running and coaching place demands on athletes and coaches which are very great. Planning is essential and can contribute greatly to success.

25

HOW WELL DID THEY RUN?

Carl Greenhut,
Lindenhurst, L.I., New York, High School

Usually, when a cross-country race is over, the coach checks the times and place positions of each of his runners and thereby attempts to determine how well each of the participants performed. Actually, he has seen very little of the race, and using only the criteria of time and place position, he is not able to evaluate the performances properly. Because so much of the race has been obscured from his view, his only recourse is to question the team members about what transpired out on the course. Too often the questions are hit and miss, and just as frequently the answers are vague and distorted.

Race Evaluator

We developed a questionnaire which can easily be completed in a few minutes after a race (chart 1). As shown, the contribution made by our fourth man was instrumental in gaining a 1-point championship victory in a race in which the team was seeded third at best. The questionnaire serves a two-fold purpose. It emphasizes certain achievements and skills of cross-country running which are fundamental to the habits of a winning team. Also, due to the nature of the questions asked, the questionnaire helps to motivate runners to improve their performances by giving them goals to accomplish from start to finish. Our runners develop maximum effort and winning skills by demonstrating their ability to show desire and concentration in key segments of the race. In addition, since a perfectly run race is rare, the questionnaire gives each runner a chance to state how he can improve his future performances.

Chart 1

Lindenhurst High School

Cross-Country Race Evaluator

Meet ___League I Championship_____ Date _____
Runner's Name ___Bob Munson_____ Time _____Place _____

Performance	Score
1. Did you defeat any opponents rated above you? (20 each)	60
2. Did you defeat any teammates rated above you? (10 each)	10
3. Did you finish in the top five?(20)	—
4. Did you score? (20)	20
5. Did you displace? (20)	—
6. Did you follow your pre-race plan? (10)	10
7. Were you in the top third of the pack at the quarter? (10)	10
8. Were you within 50 yards of the pack leader at the mile? (10)	—
9. Did you go ahead of all opponents at the mile? (10)	—
10. Did you start your kick before your opponents? (10)	—
11. Were you never passed by opponents after the mile? (10)	10
12. Did you defeat any opponents in the final sprint? (10 each)	10
Total Score	130

How can you run a better race?
   I can go up front sooner at the mile.
   I can start my kick earlier.

To begin, when a runner defeats one or more opponents rated above him, he has made a substantial contribution to the team effort. In essence, this is what competition is all about, and we want our runners to think of it as the ultimate goal. Hence, in the questionnaire, this is weighted heavily. Second, the boy who outruns a teammate rated above him will certainly have new horizons regarding the limits of his ability. In this breakthrough, which eventually serves to push the team to better performances, the accomplishment is well rewarded.

Any boy who scores in the top five of a meet, barring unusual circumstances, has run well even if things did not go quite up to expectations. His effort is of exceptional team value. Also, a boy who is one of the top five finishers on his own team is, indeed, making a great contribution to the team effort. Finally, if a boy was not one of the top five but did displace scorers of the opposition, he made a worthwhile contribution. Sometimes the efforts of the sixth and seventh men are so crucial to the final score that they should receive special recognition if they are successful in this category.

The balance of the questions are based upon winning skills from start to finish. They are within the capabilities of most boys who have had a reasonable amount of experience and training for cross-country. Obviously, a boy who hopes to be successful does not simply run as fast as he can for as long as he can. In fact, those who do run with neither goals to accomplish nor skills to concentrate upon are often tail-enders plodding along, doing little for themselves or their teams. By being aware of crucial situations, a boy has a better chance for victory, and more importantly, for preventing defeat. Therefore, we insist that each runner follow a pre-race plan, that each one attempt to get into the top third of the pack a quarter-mile from the start, and that each winner attempt to be within range of a chance for good success at the one mile mark.

At the one mile mark, the outcome of the race is already in its fnal stages. With fatigue affecting all competitors, we ask the winners to show their courage and give it a real go from this point. Finally, the contest right down to the wire is the birthplace of champions, so we ask for still one more last-ditch effort toward accomplishing the ultimate goal of a race.

Scoring, Self-Improvement

After a meet, each participant fills out his questionnaire while the race is fresh in his memory. He determines how valuable he was to the team, analyzes his strengths and weaknesses, and makes suggestions for self-improvement. A score of less than 50 points gives clues to serious shortcomings. Those runners who score from 50 to 100 points have performed adequately. A score above 100 points indicates excellent achievement. Should a boy total more than 200 points, he has run a dream race of championship calibre to the limit of his ability.

26

RUNNING THE HILLS

F. X. Cretzmeyer,
University of Iowa

Uphill Running (Series A)

The cross-country runner must expect to work harder and expend more energy when running uphill than when he is running over a flat or a down hill surface. Although he does not go into a full sprint, the runner's form must have sprinting qualities. His body lean is more forward, he has more knee-lift, his arm action is much more vigorous, and there is a greater drive and extension of the driving leg.

At each step, the runner makes a well-balanced ball-heel landing, and drives into his lean again as he rolls over his foot and into the next driving stride.

There is always a tendency for runners to let up some after reaching the top of a hill. Therefore, it is often a good tactical move to have a runner continue to work hard, for an additional 50 to 60 yards after reaching the hill's peak, in order to build up a lead over opponents who are accustomed to letting up. Building up a lead in this way often discourages opponents so that contact can be broken.

Downhill Running (Series B)

The most important work in down-hill running is relaxation. The runner's posture is more erect, with his head a bit forward so that he can check his footing, and the arm action now is definitely passive, with relaxation of the lower leg, the foot makes a heel-ball landing.

Unless the slope is extremely steep. the runner will find it less tiring to go into free wheeling and not try to hold himself back. At the bottom of the hill, the runner coasts back into his normal running style and continues at his normal pace.

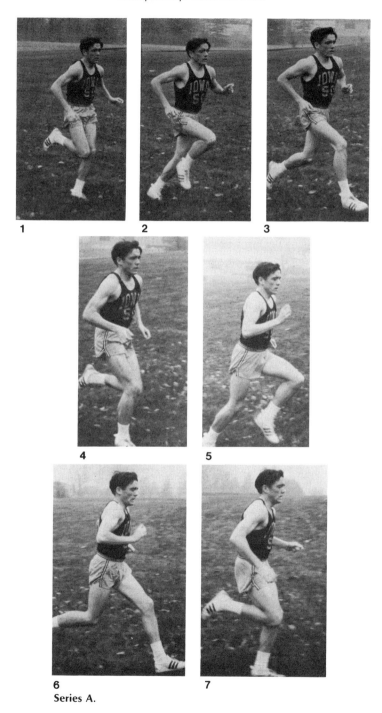

1 2 3

4 5

6 7

Series A.

1   2   3

4   5   6

7   8

Series B.

27
AN ECLECTIC TRAINING PROGRAM FOR CROSS-COUNTRY

Richard L. Marsh,
New York State University

There is little doubt, as we review the training programs of the outstanding coaches and runners, that interval training is at the heart of every successful training program. Yet outstanding runners and coaches are not so naive as to believe that interval training, that is short interval training, alone, is the secret to successful performances.[1]

We know that the Lyiard system is initiated with marathon running.[2] Igloi frequently had trials of longer distances than 400 meters when working with Rozsavolgyi, Iharos, and Tabori.[3] Sam Bell[4] at Oregon State and John Morriss[5] at Houston both incorporate longer repeat distances for pace and endurance, especially during early season. And when the interval training is implemented with the shorter distances (100 to 200 meters), the volume is usually from 20 to 40 repetitions (at slower pace with shortened rest interval), so essentially what we have is mileage, volume or quantity. Where the quality appears is the variation of such factors as shortened rest interval, that is, application of such formulae as that of Gerschler-Reindell, that 45 to 90 seconds are adequate for a rest interval for runners repeating 100 to 200 meter distances at 14 to 16 seconds and 20 to 34 seconds respectively,[6] or the reduction of the number of repetitions and an increase in pace.

It appears reasonable to conclude that any good training system for cross-country or distance runners should be eclectic - should include the best aspects of any number of present systems available. There certainly are numerous values in this procedure.

The most outstanding value of an eclectic system is that it affords variety. Providing a variety of training, distances, techniques, terrains, etc., is better calculated to retain the interest of the average American high school or college runner than the continual boredom of interval running alone.

A second factor, and probably more important than the first, is that an eclectic system allows for meeting the individual demands of a variety of different runners. Speed training alone, as Fred Foot of Toronto and Arthur Lydiard would agree, is of dubious value when one has a runner of the caliber of Bill Crothers or Peter Snell, both of whom possess the prime attribute of speed. It is the endurance training which is of more value, with speed work later in the training cycle to sharpen performances for the big meets. Yet one doubts how Dr. Ernst van Aaken[7] of Germany could completely eliminate all speed training from the regimem of Edgar Force or Roland Watschke, and achieve the results attained, considering the need for some speed training which is essential to promote oxygen debt tolerance as well as improve oxygen intake capacity. Fartlek, a reasonable facsimile of short repeat work, has been used effectively by the Europeans and is essentially what the Lydiard system employs with the 55 to 100 yard pick-ups at every 440 to 880 of a long distance run.

The most outstanding value of an eclectic system is that it affords variety.

Cross-Country

High School (Average Race Distance 2.5 Miles)		College	(4.0)
1¼	2-4 repetitions	4 mile	1-2
1	2-4 repetitions	2 mile	2-4
¾	2-4 repetitions	1¼,	
		1½,	
		1¾,	4-6
880	4-8 repetitions	1 mile	4-8

Shorter distance pace-endurance work involves:

High School			College:		
330	6-12	Paced	440	8-12(max.20)	Paced
440	6-12 (max. 20)	Paced	660	8-12	Paced
550	4-6	Paced	880	6-12	Paced
660	4-6	Paced	¾	3-8	Paced

Recommended programs for speed-endurance work:

High School			College*		
100 yards	10-20	14-16 secs.	100 yards	20-40	14-16 secs.
220 yards	8-20	30-34 secs.	220 yards	12-20	30-34 secs.
			440 yards	8-20	68-74 secs.

*Rest intervals 45 to 90 sec. easy jogging

Sample One Week Program

Monday - Twelve to 15 440s on a flat course.

Tuesday - Two miles 4 to 6 times on a golf course.

Wednesday - six to 12 330s on hills.

Thursday - Marathon running, 9 to 12 miles steady on a golf course at 5:30 - 7:00 per mile pace.

Friday - six to 8 880s on the grass, flat or rolling; (or 12 to 20 220s or 10 to 40 100s).

Saturday - Five to 15 miles easy running or Fartlek.

Sunday - Rest or 5 to 10 miles of steady running.

A third factor is the efficacy of an eclectic program in conditioning the organism to react to a variety of stimuli efficiently such as fast pace, slow pace; hill running, flat running, sand running; steady running with occasional bursts for passing; and strenuous workouts alternated with days of recuperation running.

An eclectic program for cross-country and distance runners should initially involve a period of easy cross-country running and subsequent Fartlek to prepare the runner for more strenuous interval training, repetition running, time trials, etc. This initial period for American high school runners or college runners should begin in the middle or late summer, for cross-country; during the interim between the end of cross-country and the beginning of outdoor track (no later than January, but preferably November or December) for the outdoor track runner. A reasonable length of time is six to eight weeks.

It is during this period that the marathon system of Arthur Lydiard seems appropriate. The runner should begin on a time or mileage basis, initially attempting to run for a longer period of time at each outing, without regard for mileage; later building up to a mileage averaging 8 to 15 miles at an outing with an initial pace of 7:00 per mile. As the distance increases, in early season marathon running, the pace will increase; as the distance decreases, the pace should decrease to 6:30, 6:00, and eventually by season's end (cross-country) 5:00 and under for shorter distances.

Early season interval work should be principally of three types: longer distance pace-endurance work, shorter distance pace endurance work, and shorter distance speed-endurance work.

Bibliography

1. Wilt, Fred. "Training Trends in Distance Running,"*Scholastic Coach,* Vol. 33, No. 6, February 1964.

2. Doherty, Ken. "Distance Training the Arthur Lydiard Way," *Scholastic Coach,* January 1964.

3. Mulak, Jan. "Mihaly Igloi's Training Methods," *Track Technique,* No. 8, June 1962. Track and Field News, Los Altos, Calif., pp.228-231.

4. Bell, Sam. "Cross-Country," *NCAA Track and Field Clinic Notes,* Ann Arbor, Mich., 1963, pp.14-18.

5. Morriss, John. "Distance Running," *NCAA Track and Field Clinic Notes,* 1963, Ann Arbor, Mich., pp. 19-24.

6. Gerschler, Woldemar. "Interval Training," *Track Technique,* Track and Field News, Los Altos, Calif. No. 13, September 1963, pp. 391-396.

7. Van Aaken, Ernst. "Speed or Endurance Training," *Track Technique,* Track and Field News, Los Altos, Calif., No. 1, Sept. 1960, pp.3-6.

8. Stampfl, Franz. *Franz Stampfl on Running,* Wyman and Sons, Ltd., London, 1956.

28
A WEIGHT TRAINING PROGRAM FOR DISTANCE RUNNERS

John Randolph,
Head Coach, University of Florida

Strength is a vital requirement for the successful distance runner.

In formulating a prototype of the ideal distance runner's physical characteristics, we are not implying that an upper body of muscle beach proportions is the goal. Instead, we are seeking to design a training program that will produce the *strength of constitution* necessary to survive the volume of training mileage which most distance runners feel they need to undertake to succeed.

We establish two goals for our runners in setting up our weight training program: (1) Injury prevention and (2) upper body strength.

Our injury prevention exercises are done with the idea of building up critical areas of the body that experience has shown us are vulnerable.

Upper-body strength is desired because of the stability and finishing drive it can produce during a race. The arms, chest and abdomen are all active in running and are often overlooked and consequently underdeveloped. We feel that these areas of the body should be toned up to compliment the runner's lower body musculature, movement, and rhythm.

In devising our weight training program, we are concerned with the gradual, long-range buildup of our runners. Three to five pounds of coordinated muscle development over the course of a year is an adequate strength gain that can be an asset for the runner throughout his competitive career.

It is also important to remember that weight training should not become an end in itself. Weight training is a secondary training aid which is done after the primary practice activity (running) has been completed.

The primary objective of a properly-organized weight training program is to make the athlete as "injury-free" as possible.

During the fall and early winter, our runners lift three times weekly (Monday, Wednesday and Friday) at the end of the practice session. From mid-indoor and during the outdoor seasons we lift only twice weekly.

Our strength development program takes about 15-20 minutes. Along with our weight training routine, we spend time doing static stretching to produce (and restore) greater muscle flexibility. This is a key to an effective weight training program and is a great aid in injury prevention as well.

Our most popular stretching exercises include the Achilles stretch from a leaning position against the wall, the hurdlers layout position on the floor, and various ankle flexibility and resistance exercises. We do these daily before and after the running portion of the training session.

The weight training exercises can be done with free barbell weights set up at various stations or by utilization of a weight lifting machine. We encourage our athletes to keep track of their progress either by means of a weight card or a simple chart on the wall. Either way, the goal is growth and increased strength over the course of the seasons.

The program below represents a typical fall "lifting day." These exercises are not set forth in any prescribed order; that is left to the individual.

As in any phase of coaching, the success of your weight program will depend on your ability to teach your athletes the proper lifting techniques and upon your supervision to ensure safety and progress.

The hour you devote weekly to weight training can pay great dividends for your runners as they turn an old weakness into new strength and confidence.

Exercise	Objective(s)	Weight	# Sets	#Repetitions*
1. Toe Raisers	1. Prevent shin splints	Heavy	1	20-30
(Wt. on shoulders)	2. Strengthen gastroc, achilles tendons, ankles	⅔ body weight		
2. Leg Raise (seated on bench, leg dangling off end	1. Strengthen quadriceps 2. Increase knee stability	15-25 lbs.	1 set each leg	10-14 repetitions- count to 10 with leg straight in last "rep"
3. Military Press	1. Build up arms	60-90 lbs**	2	10-14
4. Bench Press	1. Build up back	75-125 lbs**	2	10-14
5. Curls	1. Upper body drive 2. Balance, stability, endurance	40-75 lbs**	2	10-14
6. Situps (inclined board- rotate by touching elbow to opposite knee)	1. Build up abdomen, fore-thigh muscles	Optimal - 5-10 lbs. at most	1	20-30

*Lower number is first session. Add 2 reps per set per workout to maximum number of reps, then add 5 or 10 lbs. and start at lower # of reps. Repeat building process over and over again.

**Starting weight should be determined by whatever weight the athlete can lift 10 times without over-extending himself. The weights with which your athletes work will depend largely on their experience and body type.

PART V

THE RELAYS

29

RELAY RACING

John W. Morris
University of Houston

There are three prerequisites for producing a good relay team. One, it is necessary to have at least five or six boys ready for competition. Two, these boys must take care of their bodies. Three, they must realized how sacred the baton is to a championship team.

Relay events are becoming more popular every day. An illustration is that the NCAA (to be held in 1964) and the U.S.Federation (1963) voted the 440 relay and the mile relay into their national meets.

For many years the state of Texas encouraged these races. Over 1400 Texas high schools are taking part in track and they all have 440 and mile relay teams. This means that approximately 6000 boys in five high school classifications are running on relay teams, competing in from eight to twelve meets each spring. Each division will qualify eight 440-yard relay teams and eight mile relay teams for the state meet. Each of these races attracts thousands of spectators, who show their enthusiasm by rising to their feet and screaming for their favorites.

At the present time, every major meet in the United States tries to attract the top relay teams each year as a drawing card.

Relay exchanges have many variations which have been used for a number of years. We have taught our boys a little different version here and there, and feel they get everything possible out of each exchange. The method used in making an exchange does give them some advantage in certain instances.There are two types of relay exchanges: Visual - where the outgoing runner turns and takes the baton from the incoming runner. Here the responsibility for a good exchange is placed on the outgoing runner. Blind - or Non-Visual Exchange - the responsibility is on the incoming runner.

With these thoughts in mind, we will go into the mechanics of what a coach has to do to get his boys ready to function as a good relay team.

The visual relay exchange has many variations, but there are two distinct versions which most coaches use. One or the other is used on all mile, two mile, distance medley, and four-mile relays.

First Version. The exchange from the left hand to the right hand - with the back of the outgoing runner toward the inside pole of the track is shown in Series A.

1

2

Series A.

Second Version. We saw the indoor exchange for the first time in 1931 at Madison Square Garden. The baton is taken in the left hand by the outgoing runner and is handed to him by the incoming runner with his right hand (Series B).

1

2
Series B.

Use of the second version of the relay exchange provides many advantages. In the mile relay and all distance relays, the outgoing runner faces the pole of the track, which gives him a better view of the race.

● An outgoing runner uses a *go* mark, which varies from 13 feet to 17 feet. He must adjust his outgoing speed with the speed of the incoming runner. The longer the race, the slower will be the take-off needed for the outgoing runner. Correct *go* mark and good judgement of the incoming speed of the runner are very important.

● All outgoing runners can look to the inside and see the total race better than when they are looking over the right shoulder.

● There is less chance of being knocked down or off the track in an indoor mile relay exchange.

● It is just as easy to teach a relay man to start with his left foot back as it is for him to use his right foot back. We start to teach a boy these exchanges when he is a freshman.

● A relay man can run with the baton in either hand during the race; however, we prefer that he run with the baton in his right hand until he gets a pole position. This method lessens the possibility of the baton being knocked out of his hand.

Our set rule on the exchange is: Carry the baton in the right hand. Give it to the outgoing runner in his left hand. Following this procedure definitely gives the runner a better picture of the race. He can adjust himself better as to where the pole of the track is, which will enable him to feel the pulse of the race better in getting to the first curve.

In the non-visual or blind exchange, the responsibility is placed on the incoming runner. This exchange is used by all 440- and 880-yard relay teams.

Three distinct variations are used quite commonly, although there are at least six variations of exchanging the baton. Hip exchange - used many years ago. Palm back exchange - used by about 95 per cent of the relay teams. Palm up - the University of Houston has used this exchange for many years and we feel it definitely helped us.

First Version. The first runner starts with the baton in his right hand, gives it to the second runner who receives it in his left hand. Then the second runner immediately changes the baton from his left hand to his right hand runs to the third man, who also takes the exchange in his left hand and immediately changes it to his right hand. The fourth relay man also takes the baton in his left hand and usually runs through the finish with it in his left hand - right, left, right, left, changing hands after the exchange (Illustration C).

Second Version. The number one man starts with the baton in his left hand gives it to the second man in his right hand. He immediately places the baton in his left hand and runs to the third runner, who also takes the baton in his right hand and immediately changes it to his left, runs to the fourth runner who takes it in his right hand, and runs through the finish - left, right, left, right, changing hands.

Third Version. The third type of exchange is where the number one runner starts with the baton in his right hand. He gives it to the second runner in his left hand. This runner takes the exchange in his right hand and runs with it in his right hand. Then the anchor man takes the baton in his left hand and completes the race.

Fourth Version. The first runner starts with the baton in his left hand; the sprinters do not change hands after each exchange, but the baton is changed from man to man using the left to right - right to left - left to right. The exchange version is right foot back, looking over the right shoulder.

Fifth Version. The first runner starts with the baton in his right hand. Then the second runner takes the exchange in his left hand - palm up. This procedure is repeated right, left, right, left - palm up and then they change hands.

We definitely feel that versions one, two, and five in which the runners change hands with the baton, cannot be executed as well as when the runners do not change hands. Our primary reason is that when a sprinter changes hands it takes at least two strides; therefore, he is not running with any arm-power, thereby losing time.

Illustration C.

174

Sixth Version. This version is similar to the fourth only in that the exchange is from left to right, Series D, left to right, Series G, right to left. Illustration E shows the lead-off man in the "set" position in his blocks. Notice the method of gripping the baton.

In these exchanges, the runners use the palm up for all baton passes. We also have all of our sprinters start with the left foot back and looking to the inside. As shown in Illustration F, the man who is about to take the baton is looking to his inside over his left shoulder and has started his left leg drive for his first stride. We have used this exchange since 1959 and feel these two new additions, palms up and left foot back, have helped us tremendously.

Notice the position of the baton in Illustration D4 as the exchange is completed. In this illustration, the runner is ready to pull with his arms and does not have to get the baton in position for the next exchange as it is in perfect position with the palm-up exchange. The exchange is completed at about the 17 yard point.

As shown in Series G, the incoming runner checked up. He had to slow down for the exchange. The trouble here was caused by the number three man who started soon enough, but not fast enough. Notice particularly the error in Illustration G2 where the back of the hand should have been more parallel to the track. The next illustration shows the outgoing runner attempting to take the baton instead of letting the incoming runner give it to him. Illustration G4 clearly indicates what happens when the baton is too high up in the palm of the hand, thus requiring that it be pulled up into better position for the last exchange.

We feel that in our type of relay exchanging, the key runners are the number one and number three boys. Our reasoning is that if we have ten potential sprinters, about three of them, on the average, will run into a curve very well. The other seven boys run better out of a curve. In many instances, a great deal of time is spent teaching a boy how to run into a curve and when to start his drift for the number one or the number three exchange.

We feel that if we have four sprinters who can run 9.7, 9.8, 9.9, and 10.0, they should run 41.0 or better if they are hitting their exchanges with any degree of accuracy.

Our blind exchange has helped us tremendously. The exchanges shown in the preceding illustrations are from the number one man to number two and from the number two man to number three, showing body and hand positions.

The number two and number four boys stand in the outside of their lanes with the left foot back, running out of the curve. These two boys try to run a straight line on an angle to the middle of the exchange zone.

The number one and number three boys start their drift on exchanges number one and number three in two ways:

● By straightening the body up slightly on the curve as they hit the inside border of the exchange zone.

1

2

3

4
Series D.

Illustration E.

Illustration F.

1   2

3   4

Series G.

- By not pulling so hard with the inside arm and letting the curve throw them to the outside for the exchange.
- On the number one and number three exchanges we try to go through the bisect at about 13 or 14 yards in the exchange zone.
- The exchange is made at about 15 to 18 yards.
- The number two exchange is made by the second runner running the inside one-third of his lane. The number three man should run the middle one third of his lane until the exchange is made.

Relay Starting Positions. All of our boys start from different positions. They vary from 17 feet to 22 feet, depending on how fast each boy can start. The distance has to be worked out using many exchanges in practice. These starting positions on relays are marked with grass, sawdust, flour or salt so the boys will not make a mistake in starting too soon or too late and can see their starting mark plainly.

All exchange versions where the runner looks over his right shoulder to see the incoming runner must start with the right foot forward.

The 880 Relay Exchanges. These exchanges may be any of those previously mentioned. The one big difference is where the outgoing runner starts. This go checkpoint should not be over 13 to 17 feet, depending on the speed of the incoming runner and the start of the outgoing runner.

International Rules. International relay exchange zone rules will be used in Texas Federation meets. The IAAF zone will also be used on other Federation meets this year. This zone was used for the first time in the 1963 Sugar Bowl meet and the coaches liked it very much. The zone differs from the normal zone in this way. The NCAA zone is 20 meters in length; the IAAF zone is 30 meters, or about 31 yards. A relay exchange must be made in the regular 20 meter zone. The baton cannot be exchanged in the first 11 yards. Last summer the U. S. team was disqualified in the meet with Russia, because its exchange was made in the first 11 yards.

Because this zone is used in the Olympics and other international competition, it is to our advantage to switch to this type of zone. We should try to conform to as many of the IAAF rules as possible.

This zone will also help in three other ways: 1. An athlete will have more momentum in the additional 11 yards. 2. The relay men can relax and make a better exchange. 3. The 440 times will be approximately five-tenths of a second faster.

Do's and Don'ts of the Relay Exchange

Mistakes made by relay racers in exchanging and running relays are:

● They should exchange enough to have confidence in each relay member.

● Have a runner always run in the same position.

● Sprinters anticipate too much before leaving check marks.

● They do not have their feet placed well enough for balance. By leaning too much they are often off balance when starting.

● They do not talk to one another enough on exchanges. We use check marks for starting, for the hand throw back, and talking commands.

● Often a runner wears glasses. Then he has poor judgement of distance, which hurts him in starting too soon or too late. When possible, use him as number one man.

● Incoming runners do not run through the exchange; they ease up to make the baton pass.

- Outgoing men often start too soon, but not fast enough; or too fast, too soon.
- Judgement of distance and timing plays a very important part.
- In the 440 and 880 relay exchanges, the incoming runner should keep his eyes on the outgoing runner's exchange hand until the exchange is completed.
- The outgoing sprint relay man should never try to take the baton until he feels it is firmly in his hand.
- A good relay runner has to think all the time.
- A boy who is thinking about his girl, the crowd, grades, parents or financial troubles is better off in the stands.
- Our relay men practice 440 relay exchanges twice a week. These number from six to twelve total exchanges.
- In the 440 and 880 relays, the responsibility for the exchange is placed on the incoming man.
- We start to get out boys ready when they are freshman and then fit them into positions where they stay.
- A boy who can only run 10.1, but is a good double exchange man, is more valuable than a 9.7 man who cannot take exchanges or think clearly.

Mile Relay Exchanges

1. We have our incoming runner carrying the baton in his right hand. He tries to accelerate all he can for the exchange, and attempts to run through the exchange.

2. The outgoing man takes the baton with his left hand. He has a check mark of between 13 to 17 feet for the start on the incoming man. When the outgoing man starts, he runs about three strides, not more than eight to ten yards, then looks back to make the exchange.

3. The worst things that can happen in mile relay running are: The incoming runner ties up. The incoming runner turns the baton loose before he is sure the outgoing runner has it. The outgoing runner leaves too soon. The outgoing runner stands flat-footed, and has the incoming runner run over him

The Shuttle Hurdle Relay

In the early 30's the shuttle hurdle relay became a popular race. Competition is run with four hurdlers. Each runner runs 120 yards of hurdles in shuttle fashion. The number one and number three hurdlers will run to the north on the track. The number two and number four hurdlers will hurdle down the track to the south.

Various tag-offs which have been used are: the hand tag, hip tag, shoulder tag, and now the box system. The box system has been used recently and seems to be the most practical. The Drake Relays placed this on their program in 1960 at the suggestion of the coaches.

Let us assume that team one is in lanes number one and number two. The hurdlers in lanes one, three, and five. The hurdles are then set running south for hurdlers in lanes two, four and six. Team number two will be in lanes number three and four. Team number three will be in lanes number five and six.

Notice the eight-foot starting line shown on the track at the left of illustration H1. Illustration H4 shows both hurdlers perfectly in the four-foot box.

1

2

3

4

Series H.

In order to exchange correctly and be legal, all hurdlers must be inside the four-foot box on each end. Thus it is easy for one judge on each end of the exchange to judge the shuttle race, This method has worked very well in the last few years with a minimum of disqualifications. It also helps the hurdler concentrate more on his hurdle race, which is difficult enough to do because his mind is relieved of all hand tags. Years ago, it was necessary for a judge to hold on to an outgoing hurdler because the hurdler, in his excitement, often forgot to tag his outgoing partner's shoulder as he ran by, thereby disqualifying his team.

With the four-foot box the responsibility is placed on the athlete and not on the judge.

Suggested movement on the shuttle hurdle exchanges where the four foot box system is used is as follows:

- The number one hurdler should start and run his regular race.
- The number two hurdler should place one mark down in the number one hurdler's lane at 35 feet. The second mark should be placed at eight feet in the number one lane. Both of these marks should be close to his lane.

The number two hurdler should stand behind his blocks until the number one hurdler comes off the eighth hurdle, at which time he goes to his marks. When the number one hurdler comes off his tenth hurdler and hits the first mark of 35 feet, the number two hurdler then assumes a *get set* position. When the number one hurdler hits the second checkpoint of eight feet, the number two hurdler starts. If he does not go early, or anticipate, both boys will be within the four-foot box and a legal exchange has been performed.

This procedure should be repeated between two to number three and from the number three to number four hurdles.

30

IMPROVED TECHNIQUES IN SPEED RELAY BATON EXCHANGES

Richard A. Larkin,
Upper Arlington High School, Columbus, Ohio

We shall describe the speed relay baton passing pattern which has been used by many teams over the years and is very popular at the present time. Many other forms and styles have also been used in the past, and at every track meet we see a number of different techniques employed in baton exchanges.

It is difficult to account for this diversity since most of the track and field techniques are standardized.

The art of baton passing merits more attention than it now receives because no single track performance must be mastered by so many participants.

Several different terms are used by coaches of track teams to identify the passing patterns used in exchanging a baton in relay racing. Thus, sprint relay pass, blind pass, fast pass, and open pass are terms that are heard to identify the speed relay passes which are used in relay races of the 440, the 880, the mile, and the medley running races.

Distant relay pass, visual pass, slow pass, and closed pass are used to identify the pass patterns used in the two-mile, four mile, and the medley races, where the incoming runner comes to the passing zone at a controlled pace.

We will deal primarily with the sprint relay passing pattern.

The speed relay pattern of baton passing we are discussing requires a left to right execution between runners, followed immediately by a front body pass of the baton by the receiver. Thus, the baton is carried all but a few feet in the left hand by most of the team members. The first runner takes his mark with the baton in his left hand. The last runner may or may not carry the baton in his left hand.

It should be mentioned that if the exchange pass has been made properly and the cross-body pass executed correctly, half of the baton will always be untouched. Sometimes dropped batons can be attributed to the availability of only one quarter of the stick for passing purposes.

Throughout the passing and carrying period a natural and normal arm swing should always be maintained. This arm carriage allows the baton carrier to focus his eyes on the receiving hand of the next runner. When executing a pass, this arm arangement avoids positioning the arm and body at a critical moment. Furthermore, this pattern of passing allows most of the responsibility of execution to be placed on the incoming runner. This pattern seems to be valid because the incoming runner's race is almost over; he has only one additional responsibility - to hit the outstretched hand of the next runner.

The receiver should take a standing side position in the assigned lane with his body turned towards the outside lane. In this position, the runner should place his right foot nearer the zone line and in a normal stance for right-handed individuals. Standing almost flat-footed, resting his hands on his knees, and looking across his shoulder, the receiver should focus his eyes upon the incoming runner. This position should be maintained until the incoming runner touches a go mark which has been selected earlier. The go mark should be selected after considerable study and measurements. It will neither be the same spot nor the same distance from the zone line for all exchanges.

Upon seeing the baton carrier hit the go mark, the receiver should turn and face down the track. His turn is also a part of a running start and should be executed by swinging both arms in a normal manner. The arm swing should be continued for three running strides. Having executed not fewer than three running strides, the receiver's arm, which will be his right arm, should be dropped and extended back from his body. The extended arm should be locked into position by pressing it tightly against the body at the armpit. This should present a stable target to the baton-carrier.

Throughout the execution of the previously mentioned movements, the receiver's hand should always be carried in a normal manner. Upon extending his arm backward from his body, the receiver's thumb and fingers should be in a wide V position, thereby providing a cradle for the about-to-be-received baton.

If the two runners have timed their passing correctly, the incoming runner should place the extended half of the baton into the receiver's hand with an upward movement.

The final phase in the execution of the speed relay pass comes when the receiver executes a front body pass of the baton and places the lower half in his left hand, thus making it ready for the next exchange.

In order to give and receive the greatest benefit from the speed passing

1

2

3

4

5

6

7

8

9

10

11   **12**

patterns, it has been our experience that the pass should be made in the first 10 yards of the allotted zone.

Passing and receiving the baton at this place in the zone can be taught easily by having the receiver, upon turning his face and body down the track, count 1-2-3. At the count of three or four, and not later than five, the baton should have been placed in the hand of the receiver.

This count does two things: 1) The number three indicates the proper time to extend the receiving arm and place the hand in a position for the reception of the baton. 2) If the baton has not been received in the outstretched hand upon the count of five, trouble may be present.

Receiving the baton on the count of three will result in a well-executed pass as far as appearance and speed are concerned.

Speed baton passing is a learned activity and the best time to teach and coach this pattern is when the squad members are agile and wide-awake. Thus, the best period is immediately after the warm-up exercises have been completed and before starting the time trials or the interval running work of the day.

Speed baton pass work provides an all-purpose routine for most track team members. In addition, it can also be used for conditioning work. Team identity is provided during practice work, as in meet participation, and baton passing is fast becoming a technique that must be learned by more members of the squad than any other activity.

These are some of the reasons we have adopted a single style and pattern of baton passing for all relay teams at our school. Furthermore, the pattern is simple in form, easily coached, has good appearance, and is a challenging technique to learn and execute.

31

MILE RELAY STRATEGY

Tom Ecker,
Cedar Rapids, Iowa, Community Schools

Because it is the final event in most track meets, the mile relay often means the difference between winning or losing a close meet.

Many coaches feel that if they have four good quarter milers on their squad, they automatically have a good mile relay team. Consequently, they work their four relay men in an effort to lower their individual 440 times but often neglect the relay itself.

But the mile relay is more than just four quarter miles put together. There are other phases of relay racing in which a well-coached team can improve its overall relay time. Coaches who neglect this fact are greatly underestimating the importance of the mile relay as an event. By knowing and practicing the different phases of relay racing itself, the members of a mile relay team can turn in the times they are capable of running, as well as employ other less obvious skills to win the races that might otherwise have been a toss-up.

In the mile relay, many yards can be gained through smooth, efficient baton exchanges. A mediocre mile relay team with good baton passes can often defeat a team of better quarter milers whose exchanges are poor.

The baton is passed within a 20 yard zone - 10 yards on either side of the incoming runner's finish line. When he is getting ready for the exchange, the outgoing runner should wait until the incoming runner reaches a point four to seven yards away from the front of the zone where he is standing. Then he should dig out at top speed for seven steps and throw his right hand back to receive the baton, looking back over his right shoulder as the same time. His arm should be straight and his thumb and forefingers pointed downward to form an inverted V - the incoming runner's target. Ideally, the exchange is completed when both boys are running at near top speed.

Headwork is just as important as passing technique. If the incoming runner begins to falter in his final stretch run, it is the responsibility of the outgoing runner to complete the exchange with a minimum of lost time and yardage. Usually, this involves waiting an extra moment and receiving the baton in the front half of the zone. On the other had, if the incoming runner has a strong finish, the outgoing runner can use the whole zone and get a very fast exchange. Although the incoming runner is responsible for letting his teammate know verbally if the exchange is too fast, the burden of responsibility is on the outgoing runner.

It is the responsibility of the incoming runner to get the stick into the hand of the outgoing runner. The outgoing runner should never grab for the baton, but should hold his receiving hand as steadily as possible until the baton is placed in it. It is very difficult to pass the baton into a hand that is grasping for it.

Normally, the baton is handed off with the left hand, received with the right hand, and is immediately switched to the left. However, when passing on curves, as is often done on odd-length tracks, a smoother and faster exchange can be made by handing off with the right hand and receiving the baton with the left hand.

To develop baton exchange timing, the mile relay team should practice baton passing regularly. The practice can be worked into the regular workout schedule by having the boys run repeat 220's in an endless relay at quarter-mile speed. Or perhaps a few minutes could be set aside for baton passing at the end of each workout session.

Another way to cut valuable seconds off mile relay times is by reshuffling the team's running order, so that each boy is running the leg which will contribute most to the total effort. Close races that might have been lost can often be won by the boys who are running in an order based on their individual running abilities.

When deciding the order in which the boys should run, many factors should be considered. If the team is made up of a group of front runners, it would probably be best to start the fastest quarter miler first to get the team out ahead, and let the second fastest run the anchor leg. However, a team of competitors would probably run a better relay by leading off with the slowest man and working up to the fastest man for the final leg.

The two most important positions as far as selecting the team's running order are the lead-off and the anchor legs. Many teams like their lead-off man to be a fast starter. But, if there is not a runner on the team who has a fast enough start to get out in front of the pack at the beginning of the race, the first man should be one who can take any first lap jostling that might occur in the pack. Or, out of necessity, a boy might be put in the lead-off spot

The mile relay is more than just the sum of all of its parts.

because he is not as adept at receiving the baton as the others on the team.

As far as selecting an anchor man, a coach should look for the boy who can always run a little faster when the chips are down. If often takes a real competitor to pull a close relay race out of the fire.

When the team's members have the mechanics of the relay in mind, and when the best possible running order has been decided, the boys must get out and practice. Only through conscientious practice can a relay team gain the perfection that will pay off in the meets. Besides working on baton exchanges, the boys should practice carrying the baton as they run through their regular workout schedule. The lead-off man should spend some extra time driving out of the blocks with the baton in his hand, so this will not be an unfamiliar experience for him.

The mile relay is more than just the sum of all of its parts. By knowing and practicing the different phases of the event, and by running the team's individuals in the order that will produce the best results, many yards can be gained on opposing teams. An intelligently coached relay team has a decided advantage over the team made up of quarter milers who are not using good relay technique.

When a track coach is faced with a situation where the outcome of a meet depends upon the performance of his mile relay team, the event suddenly becomes more than just an afterthought. By using a little forethought, he can be confident that his well-prepared relay team will be better able to turn in a winning performance.

ABOUT THE AUTHOR

Currently the head track and field coach at the University of Florida, John Randolph has compiled a varied and outstanding record of success on the collegiate, national, and international levels. From 1976-1980, he was the chairman of the NCAA Track and Field Rules Committee. He has also served as a member of both the AAU and Olympic Development Committees. Currently, he is the chairman of the Men's Olympic Development Committee for the preparation period leading up to the Los Angeles Olympic Games. In 1977 he was head coach of the USA National Junior Team that scored impressive wins over USSR in both men's and women's competition, and in 1978 he coached the Eastern Team in the first National Sports Festival in Colorado Springs.

From 1976 until his appointment at Florida, Randolph had been head coach at the U.S. Military Academy where his West Point teams posted an excellent 54-4-1 record, including two unbeaten indoor teams. He coached seven all-Americans and developed numerous Academy record holders. In 1978 his entire cross country team qualified for the NCAA championship.

A 1964 graduate of William and Mary, Randolph returned to his alma mater in 1968 as an assistant coach while earning a master's degree in Educational Administration and Physical Education. The following year he was named head coach of the Tribe and proceeded to lead them to a record 52 championships in cross country, indoor and outdoor track in Southern Conference and Virginia Intercollegiate competition. In nine years his teams won eight Southern Conference cross country and indoor track titles, and seven outdoor crowns.

While at the Virginia school he coached 11 all-Americans, three NCAA individual champions (Juris Luzins and Reggie Clark in the 800; Howell Michael in the 1500), and four USA National Team members. He was named Southern Conference Coach-of-the-Year in cross country, indoor and outdoor track in both 1975 and 1976, and was named NCAA District 3 Southeast Coach-of-the-Year in 1972 for indoor track and 1973 for cross country.

Randolph earned two letters in cross country and six in track while an undergraduate at William and Mary, competing in the 220, 440, and 880. He won the Southern Conference in the 440 and was a member of the mile relay team, and was named the school's "Outstanding Senior Athlete" upon graduation.